Cases in Managerial Accounting: Fundamentals

Edited by Eldon J. Gardner
Accounting Education Resource Centre
University of Lethbridge

DEDICATION

This book is dedicated to Lynda and Keri whose efforts and encouragement made it possible.

Cases in Managerial Accounting: Fundamentals

Edited by Eldon J. Gardner
Accounting Education Resource Centre
University of Lethbridge

John Wiley & Sons
Toronto New York Chichester Brisbane Singapore

Copyright © 1990 by John Wiley & Sons Canada Limited

All rights reserved. No part of this work covered by the copyrights hereon may be reproduced or used in any form or by any means—graphic, electronic or mechanical—without the prior written permission of the publisher.

Any request for photocopying, recording, taping or information storage and retrieval systems of any part of this book shall be directed in writing to the Canadian Reprography Collective, 379 Adelaide Street West, Suite M1, Toronto, Ontario M5V 1S5.

Care has been taken to trace the ownership of copyright material contained in this text. The publishers will gladly receive any information that will enable them to rectify any reference or credit line in subsequent editions.

Canadian Cataloguing in Publication Data

    Main entry under title:

    Cases in managerial accounting: fundamentals
    Result of a competition sponsored by the Accounting
    Resource Centre, University of Lethbridge in 1988.
    ISBN 0-471-79517-8

    1. Managerial accounting — Case studies.
    2. Managerial accounting — Case studies — Competitions.
    I. Gardner, Eldon J. II. University of Lethbridge.
    Accounting Resource Centre.
    HF5657.4.C36 1990   658.15'11   C90-093789-0

Cover Design: Brant Cowie

Printed and bound in Canada by Gagne Printing Ltd.
10 9 8 7 6 5 4 3 2 1

PREFACE

This series of case books has been developed from the first Accounting Case Writing Competition sponsored by the Accounting Education Resource Centre of the University of Lethbridge. The cases in these books are based on real situations and have been developed by some of the finest case writers in the world. The editor and the authors are confident that these cases, and future books planned in this series, will prove to be a valuable addition to the pedagogy of accounting.

THE UNIVERSITY OF LETHBRIDGE

Sometimes called Canada's Centennial University, the University of Lethbridge is a small liberal arts university located in southern Alberta. Lethbridge, Alberta's third largest city, is 200 kilometres (120 miles) south of Calgary.

The University has gained a reputation as an institution with a 12.5 to 1 student to faculty ratio that allows for small classes and an intimate learning environment. Its faculty has a reputation for good teaching and increasingly ambitious research.

THE FACULTY OF MANAGEMENT

The Faculty came into existence on July 1, 1989 after operating for eight years as the School of Management. Its first Director, now Dean, Dr. George Lermer has administered its growth and development. Today the faculty number forty. Its curriculum is a blend of case teaching, skills training and academic rigour that meets the needs of under-graduate students.

THE ACCOUNTING EDUCATION RESOURCE CENTRE

The Centre was founded on July 1, 1987 and Dr. Eldon Gardner was appointed its first Co-ordinator. The bi-annual Accounting Case Writing Competition, from which a selection of cases is being published in this book, is its major undertaking. The mandate of the Centre is to develop educational materials for use in academic and professional accounting programs.

BACKGROUND TO THE CASE BOOK

The cases in this book are the best of those submitted in the Accounting Case Writing Competition of 1988. The cases have been thoroughly reviewed and edited for publication. The following individuals contributed to the reviewing process:

Dr. Daniel McDonald	Simon Fraser University
Dr. Henry Kennedy	University of Alberta
Dr. George Baxter	University of Saskatchewan
Dr. Peter Tiessen	University of Alberta
Lorne Baxter	University of Calgary (retired from Touche Ross)
Ronald Baines	University of Lethbridge (retired from Arthur Anderson)
Professor Allan Hunter	University of Lethbridge.

Eldon Gardner edited the cases with the capable assistance of Katherine (Kate) Beaty Chiste.

FINANCIAL SUPPORT

The financial resources needed to support the Centre and this case writing and publishing venture were provided by several sources:

(1) The Accounting Education Foundation of the Institute of Chartered Accountants of Alberta provided initial funding for three years.

(2) The Government of Alberta provided matching funds for this initial three years.

(3) Supplementary funding was provided by the Burns Foods Endowment of the Faculty of Management.

ACCOUNTING CASE WRITING COMPETITION

The first Accounting Case Writing Competition selected five finalists who presented their cases to a student audience in a simulated class room environment at the Kananaskis Inn in Kananaskis, Alberta in May 1988. The following prizes were awarded:

(1) The first prize of $5,000 (U.S.) was awarded to Professor David Bateman of St. Mary's University, Halifax, Nova Scotia for his case entitled **City Autoparts Distributors Limited**.

(2) The second prize of $1,500 (U.S.) was awarded jointly to Professor Cynthia Heagy of the University of Georgia, Athens, Georgia and Mr. Richard Heagy, then of Clemson University, Clemson, South Carolina for their case entitled **Dane Manufacturing Company**.

(3) Three other prizes of $500 (U.S.) each were awarded to each of the following:

Jointly to Professors Ralph Drtina and Charles Brandon of Rollins College, Winter Park, Florida for their case entitled **Winter Park Brewery Company**.

Jointly to Professors Hugh Grove and Patsy Lee of University of Denver, Denver, Colorado for their case entitled **Snafu Sports Shop**.

Jointly to Professors Jeffrey Kantor and Teviah Estrin of University of Windsor, Windsor Ontario and Professor Murray Bryant of University of Toronto for their case entitled **Flawless Tool and Manufacturing Limited**.

The judges for the final competition were:

William Stephen, Chairman of the Board of the Accounting Education Foundation of Alberta,
Dr. Ross Archibald of the University of Western Ontario, and
Dr. Michael Gibbins of the University of Alberta.

USES OF THE CASE BOOK

This case book has been designed to be used as a supplement to widely used accounting texts. The Teaching Notes contain a list of texts and cases that are linked to the various specific chapters in those textbooks.

The Teaching Note for each case is provided to assist the instructor in the use of the case and to outline the recommended solution. In some cases the actual events are known and are described. In others, no specific solution or outcome is available.

Each case has been assigned a level of difficulty as follows — simple, moderate or complex. Generally those with a narrower focus (and with less detail) are classified as simple or moderate. Complex cases usually have a broad focus and sufficient detail to provide students a rich learning opportunity.

ACKNOWLEDGEMENTS

This book has been made possible by the support and encouragement of many people, some of whose names appear in what follows.

The authors of the cases deserve praise for the quality of their initial work. All of them have described interesting and timely situations with realism and relevance for accounting education. Their imagination and creativity have provided some challenging opportunities for readers.

Dr. George Lermer, Dean of the Faculty of Management, had the initial vision of the case writing competition. His unswerving support and dedication to the program assisted, in no small measure, in its success.

The Advisory Committee to the Centre provided support and guidance and put a large amount of effort in ensuring its success. Its members were:

Dr. George Lermer, Chair
Professor Allan Hunter
Professor Lawrence Merkley
Ian Kinnell of Peat Marwick Thorne, Lethbridge and member of the Board of the Accounting Education Foundation of Alberta
Dr. Eldon Gardner, Co-ordinator.

Kate Chiste's editorial work has made these cases eminently readable without losing the flavour and direction intended by the authors.

A number of people provided secretarial and administrative assistance, including Marilyn Hawryluk, who organized the case reviewing and judging processes.

Rosemarie Gattiker assisted Kate Chiste in the editorial process. Barbara Driscoll, Carrie Kanashiro, Marlene Lapointe and Stella Kedoin typed the manuscripts.

The editor wishes to thank in particular his wife, Lynda Gardner. She painstakingly worked to develop the appropriate format and style for the cases. Her patience and persistence when faced with so many varied and different authors' styles and formats was vital to the success of these case books.

The publishers of these volumes, John Wiley & Sons Canada Ltd., and their senior publisher, Hilda Gowans, deserve credit for taking the risk of publishing these books. It is Dr. Gardner's hope, as editor, and theirs that these volumes will be a valuable addition for accounting educators and practitioners around the world. Users should find that these cases provide many opportunities for developing judgmental, analytical, decision-making and evaluative skills (JADE skills) in the context of studying accounting.

Finally Dr. Gardner wishes to thank the many academic colleagues who have offered their encouragement for this case writing endeavour.

TABLE OF CONTENTS

Case 1	Kodiak Adventures K. Boze and H. Wichmann Jr. 1
Case 2	The AKH Manufacturing Company R. Gruber 13
Case 3	Admiral's Hotels T. Cairney 23
Case 4	Frank's Locker Service (1984) Ltd. M. Fine and J. Thatcher 33
Case 5	Arriscraft Corporation H. Teall 41
Case 6	Quality Design and Print Limited W. Murphy and S. MacKenzie 47
Case 7	Western Industrial Supplies E. Gardner 61
Case 8	Mid-Western Publishing Co. V. Govindarajan 69
Case 9	Curry Limited P. Clarke 81
Case 10	TVFI Case J. Brackner 89
Case 11	The Case of the Missing Profits D. Knutson 93
Case 12	Strathcona Public School Board C. Batch, J. Fisher and J. McCutcheon 101
Case 13	Carbucal A. Carrera 111
Case 14	Jean's Place E. Gardner 117
Case 15	University of Washington Overhead Charges E. Noreen 127
	Interest Tables 147
	Glossary 159

P 12-25

CASE 1

KODIAK ADVENTURES

K. Boze
University of Alaska
Fairbanks, Alaska

H. Wichmann, Jr.
University of Alaska
Fairbanks, Alaska

The cold November sub-arctic wind cut into Rocky's thighs as he led Fred and Jeff through a berry patch on Kodiak Island, Alaska, where the group expected to find a grizzly bear, the largest carnivore on earth. Rocky, the guide, was silently cursing his torn pants when a large brown furry head poked up from the underbrush approximately 200 yards downwind.

"Great!" Rocky thought, "I still have my 100% success rate, ten years running! Downwind means trouble though."

The bear sniffed the air, certain he smelled humans; his powerful forelegs hung limply at his sides. The head disappeared, and Rocky guided the two hunters uphill trying to skirt around the bear. The head popped up again, in the same spot.

"A mellow bear," Rocky said to Jeff. "Good!"

As Rocky spoke to Jeff, Fred aimed and fired. The dust flew everywhere as the concussion from the shot disturbed the air around the hunters. Rocky's ears rang.

"No!" Rocky shouted at Jeff. "We're too far away. You don't want to wound a bear like this." Injured bears will stalk hunters and the bear's sounds indicated he had been hit. Rocky guided the group uphill anddownwind from the bear, keeping a sharp eye on where it had been. A cat and mouse game ensued, with hunters and bear stalking each other. Suddenly, the bear poked its head above the underbrush approximately 75 yards from the hunters, facing away from them.

"Good," thought Rocky. It was Fred's bear and Fred prepared to shoot again, but paused to look at Rocky. Rocky shook his head "No" and mouthed the word, "Wait." Suddenly, the bear spun around and looked Rocky dead in the eyes. The grizzly hopped from a standing position to charging run, bouncing through the brush like a porpoise through water. Rocky and Jeff aimed their rifles, palms sweating, hearts racing, their breaths condensing on their rifles. Fred waited nervously, then fired, hitting the bear in the chest. The bear snorted, but kept coming. Again Fred fired, again the bear snorted. On the third shot the bear fell, no more than 15 yards from the hunters.

THE GUIDE

Hunting has been a major part of Rocky Morgan's life for most of his thirty odd years. He was born in Alaska and became a licensed guide, allowing him to hunt for a living. His personality is typical of people living in a frontier environment: warm and helpful when a person is in need, but willing to shoot anyone who trespasses. Rocky's sole support is the camp, Kodiak Adventures, and he travels "outside" (to the lower 48 states) to market the camp's hunting trips at various hunting-related meetings. He lost the use of three fingers on his left hand during a knife fight at a roadhouse several years earlier, but shows no signs of slowing down.

Rocky is married with one daughter, age five. A personal balance sheet is provided in Appendix A.

THE BEAR CAMP

Rocky's bear camp, Kodiak Adventures, is located on Kiliuda Bay on Kodiak Island, 200 miles southwest of Anchorage, Alaska, near the point where the Aleutian Islands join the mainland. The camp was started in 1955 by Eli Mitrochin and Hal Waugh. A powerful earthquake and tidal wave destroyed the camp along with several Alaskan coastal towns in 1964, but the two men rebuilt at the same location; later, Hal bought Eli's share of the camp. In 1970 Hal died and left the camp to his wife, who later sold it to Earl Stevens.

Rocky bought Kodiak Adventures, which included one cabin and hunting rights, from Earl in 1979. In 1982, Rocky accepted a partner who provided the cash to buy the two boats and motors used to ferry hunters around the bay. The next year he built a second cabin and added a well for running water. In January 1986, he bought out his partner's interest. In July 1986, Rocky began construction of a 1,300 square foot lodge to complement the two cabins, and he bartered deer hunts for construction labour to minimize his cash outflow. He felt that the lodge would give him a competitive edge with family clientele, as most guides simply offered them used wall tents and lacked such basics as running water.

Rocky hopes to expand the operations of Kodiak Adventures. In February 1988, he accepted a Minnesota-based 10% partner for $17,000 cash and a free non-grizzly hunt each year. However, the local bank denied a loan request on the camp due to uncertainties about the camp's lease, although Rocky was told that the loan would be granted when the lease problem was resolved.

At the time Rocky bought the camp, Earl Stevens had told him the land was native-owned and a proper lease did exist. But Rocky has recently discovered that the camp is on state land and the law requires him to bid for the lease. These types of problems are very common in frontier environments since many pre-statehood land-related contracts were verbal — sealed with a handshake and enforced with a shotgun. Rocky swears that if he loses the bid, he'll burn the property down. However, a lawyer has indicated that Rocky should not have any problems establishing his right to the lease.[1]

Due to the hazardous nature of his occupation, Rocky is unable to obtain life insurance. He is also unable to obtain fire insurance on the camp buildings and equipment because there are insufficient water outlets on the premises. Since his seasonal help is contract labour, he is uncertain whether he is required to have workers' compensation insurance.

HUNTING RIGHTS

The Alaska Department of Fish and Game allots tags for grizzly bears based upon a lottery system; Rocky is allotted three fall and two spring Kodiak grizzly bear tags a year. This limits his ability to expand that portion of his hunting operations, for which there is considerable demand. In fact, he is booked for the next three years, even though he requires a 50%, non-refundable deposit.

He has just spent $5,000 to acquire the hunting rights to an area in the Brooks Range, the mountain range bordering the Arctic Sea coastal plains 100 miles north of the Yukon River. With this addition to his Kodiak Island and other nearby hunting areas near Seward, Alaska, Rocky guides hunts every month of the year except December through February (winter) and July. See Table 1 for hunting and fishing seasons with which Rocky is involved with.

OPERATIONS

Rocky Morgan runs the operations and is the "Boss." Rocky's wife, Mary, is the camp cook. His brother, Blaine, is an assistant guide for the fall hunts, but works as a commercial fisherman during the spring and summer. Two temporary assistant guides are hired during the spring brown bear season and one is hired for the fall bear hunts. A married couple takes care of the camp during winter for room and board only.

In-state hunters are charged less than out-of-state hunters partly due to differences in state laws; in-state hunters do not need guides whereas out-of-state hunters must have one.

Table 2 includes Kodiak Adventures' price list.

TABLE 1
KODIAK ADVENTURES
SEASONS FOR KODIAK ADVENTURES' GUIDES

	HUNTING	FISHING
January	Open	Open
February	Open	Open
March	Kodiak Grizzly Bear	Open
April	Kodiak Grizzly Bear	Open
May	Kodiak Grizzly Bear	Open
June	Seward Black Bear	Halibut, King Salmon
July	Open	Halibut, Red Salmon
August	Brooks Range, Dall Sheep, Moose and Caribou	Halibut, Chum, Silver and Pink Salmon
September to October 15	Seward Black Bear, Moose and Mountain Goats	Silver Salmon
October 15 to November	Kodiak Grizzly Bear and Kodiak Island Deer	Open
December	Open	Open

Note

Halibut fishing is possible all year, but for planning purposes Rocky wants to limit his offering to 13 weeks in the summer (June to August). He is assuming 17 weeks (through September) for salmon

TABLE 2
KODIAK ADVENTURES
PRICE LIST — 1988[1]

	IN-STATE	OUT-OF-STATE
Brown Bear (up to 15 days)	$3,500	$10,000[2]
Deer (limit 5)	100/day	2,000/week
Goat (limit 1)	3,500/10 days	3,500/10 days
Black Bear	negotiable	negotiable
Moose	negotiable	negotiable
Caribou	negotiable	negotiable

© John Wiley & Sons Canada Ltd. All rights reserved.

Notes

[1] *It is common to charge out-of-state hunters more than in-state hunters. State law limits Rocky's annual permits for out-of-state hunters to five brown (grizzly) bears. In-state hunters have no limits, but must have their own permit obtained from the Alaska Department of Fish and Game based on allotments to individuals estimated from population increases in grizzly bears. Hunting grizzly out of season can result in $250,000 fines and five years imprisonment.*

[2] *Rocky increased his prices from $9,000 to $10,000 per bear hunt effective January 1988.*

ROCKY'S PLANS

Rocky is trying to find financing to expand the camp after the lease problem is cleared up. Specifically, he wants to improve and expand the lodge, add more cabins, build a proper dock, buy a float plane to ferry clients from the airport to the camp, and buy a large sports fishing boat. He feels there is a large untapped market for fishing and photography trips to fill the gaps between hunting seasons and supplement his hunting income, and hopes to develop fishing first and photography later. He wants to target families, since he feels his facilities can offer the basics others do not. He has already contacted one of the cruise lines operating ships in the inland passage about offering day trips for tourists on cruise ships passing his front door.

Since Rocky has such a busy hunting schedule, he would have to bring in additional help to operate the fishing trips. He would like to run the fishing business on a percentage basis until the trips become popular enough to support someone full time. He wants to hire a person who can keep a group happy even if no fish are caught.

Rocky is very experienced in locating wildlife. He can promise visitors they will see bears, seals, sea lions, foxes, otters, ducks, bald eagles, and other wildlife near the camp. Salmon run past the camp all summer, including July when the camp is idle. The salmon spawn in the creeks and glacial lakes of the snow-capped mountains on the island. In addition, halibut fishing is excellent in the deep waters of Kiliuda Bay.

With a float plane, fishing clients could be flown over the mountains to king and red salmon fishing streams; boat travel to these spots would be too time-consuming. These two are the most highly prized salmon: the reds are considered the tastiest and the king are the largest — it is not unusual to catch king salmon the size of a small adult.

INCREMENTAL COSTS ASSOCIATED WITH FISHING

Table 3 contains Rocky's "best guess" of the incremental costs associated with adding fishing trips to his operations. Rocky is considering purchasing or leasing either a boat or sea plane, or both. He is also considering either financing the purchase with an unsecured 10% loan or seeking additional equity financing. He is not certain of the best alternative or the price to charge. He feels $1,500 per week for fishing would probably just break even; the market price is around $2,500 per week. Incremental costs and revenues would probably be similar for both fishing and photography trips.

Rocky's banker has told him that loan payments for the plane and boat would probably be[2]:

$100,000, 10%, 20 year $965.02 month
 50,000, 10%, 15 year   537.31 month

QUESTIONS

1. Should Rocky add fishing and photography trips to the operations of Kodiak Adventures? Evaluate his plans for renting versus buying the boat and/or airplane, including the probability his forecasts will be accurate. Calculate:
   a. incremental costs and revenues
   b. contribution margins
   c. break-even points for each alternative assuming full and half full trips
   d. break-even price for each alternative
   e. the probability of these estimates being accurate, for both the short and long term

2.. If Rocky approached you to become a 10% partner, what would you do? Remember that since the balance sheet was prepared Rocky has taken one 10% partner for $17,000 and a free non-grizzly hunt each year.

ENDNOTES

1. *Rocky hopes to obtain the lease from the state by May 1988. He is, as of the date of this writing, a squatter on public land — a common practice in Alaska. Hunting areas are bought and sold from guide to guide. Some guides build small log cabins which, by state law, must be left unlocked for stranded people to find shelter. Usually, people who use these squatter's cabins replace food eaten and have been known to make minor repairs to windows, doors and roofs. A guide must appeal to the state to obtain squatters' rights, which last 55 years if granted; these rights are honoured by Guides and Fish and Game Wardens as well.*

2. *The annuity method of depreciation treats the principal amount of the loan payment as depreciation; hence the cash and accrual break-even points would be similar.*

TABLE 3
KODIAK ADVENTURES
EXPECTED COSTS ASSOCIATED WITH FISHING OR PHOTOGRAPHY (in dollars)

Incremental Fixed Costs		Life (years)
Ocean going sports fishing boat and poles	50,000	15
Sea wall and dock	40,000	20
Sea plane	100,000	20
Liability insurance on boat (annual)	10,000	
Liability insurance on plane (annual)	18,000	

Incremental variable costs (per seven day trip):

Boat costs (7 day trip amounts – capacity = 6 people)

Buy:
Fuel	190	
Repair & Maintenance	175	
Crew	600	
Supplies	100	
Food	400	
Total		1,465

Rent:
Lease boat for season	15,000

Sea plane costs (7 day trip – capacity 4 people):

Buy:
Fuel	1,125	
Repair & Maintenance	275	
Pilot	1,050	
Supplies	50	
Food	200	
Total		2,700

Rent:
Hourly rental cost (with fuel and pilot) – 30 hours @ $300/hr.	9,000

Note

A smaller float plane (3 passenger seats) is available for $250 per flight hour.

APPENDIX A
KODIAK ADVENTURES
PERSONAL BALANCE SHEET FOR ROCKY MORGAN

Rocky Morgan & Family
Balance Sheet — Market Values (in dollars)
December 31, 1987 and 1986

ASSETS	1987	1986
Cash in the Bank	100	-0-
Personal Effects	12,000	10,000
Mobile Home (Wasilla – winter home)	21,000	28,000
Land in Wasilla	23,000	26,000
Equity in Kodiak Adventures	210,592	232,166
Total Assets	266,692	296,166

LIABILITIES & NET WORTH	1987	1986
Note Payable to Mobil Oil Co.	-0-	15,000
Note Payable to Credit Union	1,500	-0-
Mortgage Note on Land	15,000	15,000
Due to Doctors and Hospital	6,000	7,000
Utility Bills	-0-	1,500
Note on VCR	-0-	400
Total Liabilities	22,500	38,900
Net Worth	244,192	257,266
Total Liabilities and Net Worth	266,692	296,166

Note

Wasilla is a small modern town thirty minutes north of Anchorage on the highway between Fairbanks and Anchorage.

APPENDIX B
FINANCIAL STATEMENTS
KODIAK ADVENTURES

INCOME STATEMENT (in dollars)
For the Years Ended December 31, 1987 and 1986

REVENUE	1987	1986
Kodiak Brown Bear Hunts (5 x $9,000)	45,000	45,000
Less: Discount on Bear Hunt	1,500	-0-
Net Revenue on Bear Hunts	43,500	45,000
Deer/Black Bear Combination Hunt	-0-	2,500
Deer Hunts (5 Resident Hunts x $500)	-0-	2,500
(32 resident hunts x $500)	16,000	-0-
Total Revenues	59,500	50,000
OPERATING EXPENSES		
Advertising Expense	3,080	-0-
Booking Agent (15% of Brown Bear Hunts)	6,750	6,750
Fuel	1,500	1,500
Food	4,000	4,000
Airplane (Flying Supplies and Clients to the camp – **see note**)	19,400	5,000
Travel & Lodging (Marketing in Lower 48)	1,800	3,000
Contract Labour	9,550	4,500
Depreciation (Based Upon Market Values)	3,150	500
Telephone Expense	3,263	1,150
Radio Telephone	1,500	750
Miscellaneous (Ammunition, Spark Plugs, Salt, Licenses, etc.)	1,600	1,600
Interest Expense	462	-0-
Total Operating Expenses	56,055	28,750
Net Income (Loss) Before Extraordinary Losses	3,445	21,250
EXTRAORDINARY LOSSES		
Evinrude Motor Burned Up	(1,000)	-0-
Mercury Motor Dropped into Sea	(3,500)	-0-
Chain Saw Burned Up	(169)	-0-
VCR Burned Up	(350)	-0-
Total Extraordinary Losses	(5,019)	-0-
Net Income (Loss)	(1,574)	21,250

Note
Airplane expense increased substantially in 1987 due to Rocky's flying in sheet rock for the lodge. Rocky had experienced problems on a loan that prevented him from hiring a boat in time to bring in the sheet rock, which he had to fly in before winter arrived.

APPENDIX B
FINANCIAL STATEMENTS
KODIAK ADVENTURES
BALANCE SHEET (in dollars)
As at December 31, 1987 and 1986

ASSETS	1987	1986
Current		
Cash in the Bank	2,500	100
Accounts Receivable	22,500	27,000
Supplies	2,355	1,450
Total Current Assets	27,355	28,550
Non-Current		
Guide Areas	150,000	150,000
Buildings (see schedule)	54,100	50,500
Cars & Trucks (see schedule)	9,400	8,900
Boats and Motors (see schedule)	1,600	7,925
Miscellaneous Equipment (see schedule)	23,934	18,184
Trophies	9,000	8,000
Total Non-Current Assets	248,034	243,509
Total Assets	275,389	272,059
LIABILITIES & OWNER'S EQUITY		
Current		
Accounts Payable	16,797	12,893
Notes Payable	3,000	-0-
Total Current Liabilities	19,797	12,893
Non-Current		
Deposits on Hunts (Non-Refundable)	45,000	27,000
Total Liabilities	64,797	39,893
Capital, Rocky Morgan	210,592	232,166
Total Liabilities and Owner's Equity	275,389	272,059

KODIAK ADVENTURES
SCHEDULE OF BUILDINGS AND EQUIPMENT (in dollars)

	1987		1986	
Buildings — Old	15,000		15,000	
Less Accumulated Depreciation	14,900	100	14,500	500
Buildings — New	50,000		50,000	
Less Accumulated Depreciation	1,000	49,000	-0-	50,000
Cabin —				
Brooks Mountain Range	5,000		-0-	
Less Accumulated Depreciation	-0-	5,000	-0-	-0-
Total Buildings		54,100		50,500
Cars & Trucks	13,100		12,400	
Less Accumulated Depreciation	3,700		3,500	
Total Cars and Trucks		9,400		8,900
Boats and Motors	2,900		15,850	
Less Accumulated Depreciation	1,300		7,925	
Total Boats and Motors		1,600		7,925
Miscellaneous Equipment				
Generators	5,250		1,250	
Hunting Equipment	22,184		22,184	
Air Compressor	700		-0-	
Washer/Dryer	300		-0-	
TV, VCR & Stereo	1,000	29,434	-0-	23,434
Less Accumulated Depreciation		5,500		5,250
Total Miscellaneous Equipment		23,934		18,184

© John Wiley & Sons Canada Ltd. All rights reserved.

KODIAK ADVENTURES
CASH FLOW STATEMENT (in dollars)
For the Year Ended December 31, 1987

Operating Cash Flows		
Cash Collected from Customers		82,000
Less Cash Paid to Suppliers and Labour		49,906
Cash Inflow from Operations		32,094
Investment Outflows		
Cost to Prepare Trophies taken on Hunts		1,000
Purchase Outflows		
Truck	700	
Cabin in Brooks Range	5,000	
Miscellaneous Equipment	6,519	
Total Buildings & Equipment Purchased		12,219
Sale of Used Boat and Motor		525
Cash Outflow Due to Investing Activities		12,694
Financing		
Borrowing on Note Payable		3,000
Less Withdrawals by Owner		20,000
Cash Outflow Due to Financing Activities		17,000
Increase in Cash Balance		2,400
Add Beginning Cash Balance		100
Ending Cash Balance		2,500

REFERENCES

Belt, Brian, "Cash Breakeven Point as a Tool for Small Business Analysis," **Journal of Small Business Management**, (April 1978) pp. 27–34.

Wichmann, Jr., Henry and Harold M. Nix, "Cost-Volume-Profit Analysis for Small Retailers and Service Businesses," **Cost and Management**, (May–June 1984) pp. 31–35.

CASE 2

THE AKH MANUFACTURING COMPANY

R. Gruber
University of Wisconsin
Whitewater, Wisconsin

The AKH Manufacturing Company, Inc. was established in 1981 as a custom welding and repair shop. In 1983, the company started manufacturing hand carts for a local mail order business. Demand for the hand carts increased steadily, primarily because of the high quality of the manufacturing process and the reasonable prices of the products. By 1986, AKH offered three models of hand carts, with each model aimed at a different market segment.

Model A-7 is the deluxe model, designed and built for heavy industrial use. Model K-5 is the utility model, designed for boxes, cases, and crates, i.e., containers of similar shapes and sizes. Model H-2 is the economy model, designed primarily for residential use. A summary of each model's characteristics and specifications is presented in Exhibit 1.

The owners of AKH are concerned about the company's 1987 operating performance (Exhibit 2). Sales appear to be strong, but net income as a percent of sales is weakening and cash flows from operations are starting to tighten up.

Management has been asked to evaluate the present position of the company. Information about the 1987 direct material and direct labour costs has been summarized in Exhibits 3 and 4. Exhibit 5 and 6 summarize the 1987 overhead costs and the selling and administrative expenses. Management has also been asked to develop some operating alternatives that will improve the operating performance of AKH. After several weeks of market and production research, management has developed two strategies for consideration by the owners.

© John Wiley & Sons Canada Ltd. All rights reserved.

The first alternative would increase the selling price of each model by approximately 14% of the 1987 selling price. This would represent a significant increase from the price changes that have been made in prior years. The 1988 selling prices would then be $169, $134, and $78 for models A-7, K-5, and H-2, respectively.

The marketing department strongly opposes such a large price increase and estimated that the sales volume would drop by 3,000, 7,500 and 10,000 units for models A-7, K-5, and H-2, respectively. AKH operates in a very competitive market; the price elasticity index is very high. Management asked the production department to make some minor cost improvements to the design of each model in order to help the marketing department justify the price increases to their customers. It is hoped that these improvements would partially offset the negative reaction of the market to such a large price increase.

The production department estimated that model A-7 could be improved by using a heavier nose plate and stronger supports. The additional cost would be $1.13 in steel material and .10 hours in welding labour per unit. Model K-5 could use a stronger frame and longer support braces, at an additional materials cost of $1.76 per frame and $.39 per strap brace. These improvements to K-5 would also require an additional .05 hours in the cutting department, an additional .04 hours in the welding department, and an additional .01 hours in the shipping department. Model H-2 could be improved by using the same hand grips as the other two models and by spending an additional .03 hours in the cutting department and an additional .06 hours in the welding department. The marketing department agrees that these improvements would assist them in selling the hand carts at the higher prices, but still insists that the number of units sold would decrease by 2,000, 5,000, and 7,000 units of models A-7, K-5, and H-2, respectively. In addition, the sales commission rate for A-7 and K-5 would have to change to 5.5% of the sales value instead of being based on the sales volume in units. H-2 would remain at $5.75 per unit sold.

The second alternative would automate a large part of the production process, particularly in the cutting, welding and painting departments. The labour time in these departments would decrease as follows:

Department	A-7	K-5	H-2
Cutting	25%	20%	15%
Welding	40%	30%	20%
Assembly	20%	25%	30%

The materials cost per unit would also decrease as a result of the increased automation; i.e., increased labour efficiencies would result in fewer waste and scrap units. Any steel part described in Exhibit 3 is expected to decrease by 10% per unit for each model. In addition, the indirect material cost and the supplies cost described in Exhibit 5 would decrease on average by $.84 and $.23 per unit.

The automation would cost $2,750,000 (10-year, straight-line depreciation) and would double the general insurance and the property tax overhead costs. Interest charges would increase by $159,000 per year, and two full-time repair specialists would have to be hired (annual cost for both = $52,000) to maintain the automated equipment. Supervisors' salaries would decrease by $30,000 and AKH would no longer have to rent equipment for its production facility. Repairs and maintenance would increase by $.45 per unit produced, and the utility cost would increase by $.93 per unit produced. The miscellaneous overhead costs would decrease by the same percentage as the decrease in the direct labour costs.

Management is convinced that the quality of the hand carts will not be affected by automation of the production process. Therefore, the selling price per unit would increase by only 5% in 1988. The marketing department estimates that with a 5% price increase, sales volume will increase by 1,000, 2,000, and 5,000 units for models A-7, K-5, and H-2 respectively.

CASE REQUIREMENTS

a. Prepare a detailed contribution margin income statement for 1987. Include separate columns for A-7, K-5, and H-2, and show all of your supporting computations.

b. Compute the following ratios for 1987 and explain what each one means:

   (i) Break-even point. Express your answer in terms of total sales dollars, and unit sales volume for each individual model.

   (ii) Margin of safety ratio.

   (iii) Operating leverage.

c. Prepare a detailed analysis of the two alternatives proposed by management. Comment on how each alternative would effect AKH's operating profit, break-even point, margin of safety ratio, and operating leverage.

d. Use the cost-volume-profit relationships described in the case to determine the sensitivity of the various estimates made for each alternative.

e. Tom Reburg, a recent MBA from University of Wisconsin—Madison, looked at each alternative and decided to combine them into a third possibility. Prepare a detailed analysis of Tom's proposal. (HINT: You will first have to specify exactly how the two alternatives can be combined before proceeding to discuss the effect on operating income, break-even, margin of safety ratio and operating leverage.)

f. What other factors should be considered by the owners and management of AKH Manufacturing Company before any of the alternatives are implemented?

EXHIBIT 1
AKH MANUFACTURING COMPANY
PRODUCT SPECIFICATIONS AND CHARACTERISTICS

	A-7	K-5	H-2
Height	48"	46"	43"
Weight	34 lbs.	31 lbs.	23 lbs.
Width	15"	14"	13.5"
Nose Plate	15" x 8.5"	14" x 7.5"	13.5" x 7"
Wheels	10" x 3.50" 60–80 lbs. pressure	10" x 2.75" zero pressure	8" x 1.75" semi-pneumatic
Axle (Steel)	20.5" x .75"	19.5" x .625"	18.5" x .50"
Bearings	Steel Ball	Steel Ball	Roller
Capacity	600 lbs.	500 lbs.	300 lbs.
Shipping Weight	38 lbs.	34 lbs.	25 lbs.

EXHIBIT 2
AKH MANUFACTURING COMPANY
CONDENSED INCOME STATEMENTS (in dollars)
For the years ending December 31, 1985, 1986, and 1987

	1987	1986	1985
Sales (net)	5,940,000	4,686,000	3,323,000
Cost of Goods Sold	4,153,600	3,092,750	2,110,100
Gross Margin	1,786,400	1,593,250	1,212,900
Operating Expenses	1,306,500	1,179,150	913,300
Net Operating Income	479,900	414,100	299,600

SALES VOLUME (Units)

Model	1987	1986	1985
A-7	10,000	9,000	6,000
K-5	20,000	17,500	13,000
H-2	30,000	23,500	21,000

SELLING PRICE PER UNIT (in dollars)

Model	1987	1986	1985
A-7	149	139	129
K-5	119	109	104
H-2	69	65	57

EXHIBIT 3
AKH MANUFACTURING COMPANY
MATERIAL COSTS (in dollars)

Part Description	Number per Hand Cart	Model A-7	Model K-5	Model H-2
Nose Plate	1	2.18	1.66	1.24
Axle (Steel)	1	0.486 .54	0.432 .48	0.36 .40
Supports	2	4.18	3.72	3.34
Strap Braces	2	5.27	3.51	2.90
Tube Braces	2	1.38	1.02	.94
Frame	1	10.80	8.46	8.10
Handles	2	4.94	4.32	3.46
Wheels	2	29.40	16.96	8.06
Hand Grips	2	.38	.38	.32
Cotter Pins, etc.		.15	.15	.15
Total mc/unit		59.22	40.66	28.91
		59.166	40.612	28.87

EXHIBIT 4a
AKH MANUFACTURING COMPANY
LABOUR HOURS

Operation	Model A-7	Model K-5	Model H-2
Cut and Grind Nose Plate	.10	.08	.06
Cut and Grind Wheel Assembly	.07	.06	.04
Cut and Grind Support Assembly	.09	.08	.07
Cut and Grind Handle Assembly	.08	.07	.06
Weld Assemblies into Frame	.25	.20	.12
Clean, Prime and Paint	.10	.10	.10
Test and Package	.06	.06	.05
Total Hours per Unit	.75	.65	.50

EXHIBIT 4b
AKH MANUFACTURING COMPANY
LABOUR COSTS

Cutting & Grinding Department	$9.00/hour
Welding & Assembly Department	$12.75/hour
Paint Department	$10.50/hour
Quality Control & Shipping Department	$7.25/hour
Federal Payroll Taxes	8.5% of gross wages
Provincial Payroll Taxes	5.5% of gross wages
Local Payroll Taxes	2.0% of gross wages

EXHIBIT 5
AKH MANUFACTURING COMPANY
OVERHEAD COSTS FOR 1987 (in dollars)

Overhead Item	Cost Behaviour	Amount
Depreciation—Equipment	Fixed	175,000/year
Equipment Rental	Variable	.25/unit
Insurance—General	Fixed	80,000/year
Indirect Material[1]	Variable	4.35/unit
Indirect Labour	Fixed	100,000/year
Miscellaneous[2]	Variable	2.58/unit
Rent—Building	Fixed	180,000/year
Repairs and Maintenance	Variable	.50/unit
Supervisor Salaries	Fixed	130,000/year
Supplies[1]	Variable	2.30/unit
Taxes—Property	Fixed	35,000/year
Tools	Variable	.71/unit
Utilities[2]	Variable	2.02/unit

NOTES

[1] The budgeted amounts per unit for indirect materials and supplies are averages across the total number of units produced in 1987 (i.e., 60,000 units). Management estimates that these overhead costs are actually incurred for each model in the ratio of their respective total material costs.

[2] The budgeted miscellaneous overhead and utility costs per unit are averages across the total number of units produced in 1987 (i.e., 60,000 units). These costs are actually incurred for each model in the ratio of their respective direct labour costs.

EXHIBIT 6
AKH MANUFACTURING COMPANY
SELLING AND ADMINISTRATIVE EXPENSES FOR 1987 (in dollars)

Expense Item	Cost Behaviour	Amount
Advertising	Fixed	100,000/year
Amortization—Patents	Fixed	40,000/year
Auto	Fixed	65,000/year
Commissions	Variable	9.00/unit(A-7)
		7.50/unit(K-5)
		5.75/unit(H-2)
Depreciation—Furniture & Fixtures	Fixed	10,000/year
Dues & Subscriptions	Fixed	1,000/year
Freight Out[1]	Variable	6.50/unit
Office Supplies	Variable	.65/unit
Office Salaries	Fixed	55,000/year
Professional Fees	Fixed	24,000/year
Rent—Building	Fixed	20,000/year
Salaries—Officers	Fixed	75,000/year
Telephone	Fixed	18,000/year
Travel & Entertainment	Variable	.35/unit
Utilities	Fixed	36,000/year

NOTE

[1] *The budgeted freight out expense per unit of $6.50 represents an average charge across all models sold. The total freight charges should be assigned to the individual models in relation to their respective shipping weights (Exhibit 1).*

CASE 3

ADMIRAL'S HOTEL
PART (A)

T. Cairney
St. Mary's University
Halifax, Nova Scotia

The Admiral's Hotel, beautifully situated in picturesque Halifax, is ideally located for tourists and businessmen. The Hotel includes four divisions: the Rooms Division, the Restaurant Division, the Lounge Division, and the Pub Division. The spring months are the slowest season of the year, but since the owner of the Hotel demands strict control over operations, the management still holds weekly meetings in the spring.

Overheard at an April meeting, when the March results were being discussed:

General Manager: I'd next like to address the loss situation in the restaurant.

Rooms Manager (Mike): Bob, if you would only raise your prices, you'd be earning more money.

General Manager: That's enough, Mike. Bob, can you help us understand what is happening in the restaurant?

Restaurant Manager (Bob): Well, I know that the food costs, preparation, labour and kitchen supplies are meeting our estimates. These costs consistently approximate our planned percentages of sales. But our sales are down 14%. I have raised prices, but if I raise them any more the customers will go across the street to eat. Another thing, my waitresses say that they aren't busy...

Rooms Manager (Mike): I'm making a good profit in my division.

© John Wiley & Sons Canada Ltd. All rights reserved.

Restaurant Manager (Bob): Also, the administration charges have gone up and now greatly exceed the budget. I wonder what the big expense is in head office?

Controller: (moves uneasily in his seat).

General Manager: Mike, How have your numbers been? Have we had the expected volume this month?

Rooms Manager (Mike): As I said before, I've got a good profit in my division, and that was difficult to achieve in this down season. My theory was to raise prices, which produced a profit higher than the budget.

General Manager: And what was the volume this month?

Rooms Manager (Mike): (shuffles some papers) We had a 60% occupancy of rooms compared to a budgeted 75% occupancy.

Controller: I've got the figure here. We had 3600 room nights out of a possible 200 rooms for 30 nights. We also had an average of 2 people per room, giving 7200 people.

Rooms Manager (Mike): I think that since the restaurant can't make a profit, it should be shut down.

General Manager: You do have a point, Mike. Perhaps the restaurant should be closed during the spring.

Controller: I don't agree. The Lounge and the Pub also showed losses, and they say that their volumes were down too. Bob and I have put together a few figures, and if we could speak for a few minutes, I am sure that we can get to the heart of this problem.

General Manager: O.K.

Controller: The Controller stood up and turned on the overhead. He took out his note pad which had the following summary:

1. Variance — Reasons for Restaurant Sales
2. Break-even for Restaurant
3. Contribution Margin — Keep Restaurant Open
4. Main Problem

CASE REQUIREMENT

Assume the role of the Admiral's Hotel Controller, and make his presentation to the meeting. Show calculations, and feel free to use graphs and charts for illustrations.

Material presented to the participants prior to the meeting included the following information.

ADMIRAL'S HOTEL — PART (A)
INCOME STATEMENT (in dollars)

Rooms Division	Budget	Actual
Room Revenue	225,000	234,000
Telephone Revenue	8,100	6,480
	233,100	240,480
Expenses		
Chamber Maid Wages	33,750	30,125
Room Supplies	9,000	7,390
Linen	13,500	13,542
Telephone Rental	7,290	5,832
Building Allocation	100,000	98,760
Administration	64,300	75,000
Other	5,460	4,081
	233,300	234,730
Divisional Profit (Loss)	(200)	5,750

ADMIRAL'S HOTEL — PART (A)
INCOME STATEMENT (in dollars)

Restaurant Division	Budget	Actual
Food Sales	129,600	na
Liquor Sales	64,800	na
	194,400	167,040
EXPENSES		
Cost of Sales — Food	46,656	41,242
Cost of Sales — Liquor	20,088	16,015
Waitress & Busboy Wages	18,000	15,368
Supplies	7,776	6,680
Managers' Salaries	5,000	5,000
Dish Washing	15,552	12,441
Building Allocation	30,000	29,628
Administration	55,000	64,100
	198,072	190,474
Divisional Loss	3,672	23,434
Volume	7,200	5,760
Sales Price/unit	27	29

PART (B)

The General Manager of the Admiral's Hotel was reviewing the annual spring downturn in the occupancy of the Hotel, and the resulting slowing of the complementary products. He had just decided to keep the restaurant open when he realized that there was a problem with the Functions Department.

The Functions Department was the working unit that serviced community functions and reception needs. For instance, a company would phone the Functions booking office and request services for their annual meeting. The services typically included a reception, meeting space (along with the necessary loudspeaker system, chairs, tables, audio-visual equipment), a meal in a formal dining area, and space for a dance afterwards. Admiral's would often get related revenues, since many of these late night revellers would book a room and spend the night at the Hotel.

The General Manager reviewed the Functions Department's last quarter statements; these are reproduced in Figure 1. He realized that Dave, the Functions Manager, had previously been consistently at the high bonus rate (for bonus structure, see Figure 2). The General Manager could see that Dave was not going to achieve the Budget now, let alone earn a bonus.

The General Manager was, therefore, concerned about Dave's future efforts, and also about what had gone wrong in Functions. He made an appointment to talk to the Rooms Division Manager, Mike, (Dave's immediate superior), later that day. (For organizational structure of Admiral see Figure 3.) Note that typically in the industry, a General Manager is promoted from the Rooms side of the organization.

THE ROOMS DIVISION MANAGER

Included in the Rooms Division Manager's job description is his responsibility for the Hotel when the General Manager is out of the building. Mike had already reviewed the Functions statements only to see the profit lower than the budget. The increased expenses were liquor costs of sales, labour, and the overhead administration. Mike complained to himself that he always had to answer for the problems of Functions, yet the General Manager demanded that it have a separate manager with an independent sales staff. Mike felt that the General Manager looked to the Rooms Division Manager for solutions to the problems in Functions, yet whenever things were done right it was Dave who got the praise. He was determined to say something to the General Manager, but first he had to figure out what was wrong.

The Functions Department "purchased" their services from the Rooms Division at an amount agreed upon by the two managers. Mike recalled that for the first two months 32 people had worked in the Functions Department under such an arrangement, at a rate of $6.00/hr. For the last month of the quarter, 33 people had worked, and a new price was agreed upon at $6.50/hr^{1}. Mike, who had been with the Hotel for 10 years, felt he had made a good bargain considering that his people had not been busy at the time; but Mike also had wondered if Dave knew what he was negotiating for.

THE ACCOUNTING SYSTEM

When a company contacts the Functions Department to arrange for a reception, party, or other function, the Department forwards the name and other particulars to the Accounting Department. The Controller approves the granting of credit to the company. If he is unfamiliar with the name or unsure of the reputation he will contact the Hotel's bank to perform a credit check, which usually comes back the same day. The Controller then confirms the credibility of the client. The Functions Department may agree on its own to hold the function of any company (thereby, in effect, extending credit on its own approval), but if the Controller has previously registered the client as uncreditworthy, any subsequent uncollectible amounts are charged to the Functions Division.

When purchases are made by the Functions Division Manager, the invoices are sent to the Controller's office after being approved for acceptance, price and quantity by the Functions Manager. Payment, like the authorization of receivables, is under the control of the Controller. This relieves the Operating Manager of the financial aspects of Functions, allowing him to concentrate on its operations.

The inventory levels of liquor and basic function food items (kept frozen) are determined by the Functions Manager. He also determines the amount of equipment and the amount of floor space provided for the functions. The administration expenses include accounting and other departments as well as depreciation, taxes, insurance, etc. The increase for the quarter under consideration had resulted from the increased salaries for the General Manager, Controller, and Assistant General Manager, and increased owners' withdrawals.

THE FUNCTIONS MANAGER

Dave reviewed his quarterly report on Functions; he wasn't happy. He thought that he had been doing better. In the middle of the quarter, he had turned down a contract which had a Rate of Return of 4.5%, (annualized), because he had been earning a 5% Return on Investment up to this quarter (annualized). If he had accepted it, the lower return would have reduced the Department ROI, and he might, therefore, have earned a lower bonus.

Reviewing the report, he looked at the numbers that had changed. "Surely," he thought, "I won't be penalized for liquor costs." But he was also concerned about Labour and the Administration. He wondered why Administration was taken into consideration for his profit, when he had no control over its allocation. He noted in his diary to discuss this with the General Manager.

Dave recalled the bargaining he had to do to get the extra people during the last month. He had foregone the $6.00/hr rate and replaced it with a $6.50/hr. rate after two months. Even though the staff had worked the regular hours he had needed more of them, although he had budgeted for only 30 people.

Dave also made a note to discuss a further labour cost with the General Manager (since he knew that he would be called upon to explain the quarter's results). During the last two days of the month, he had to "purchase" the services of an additional 15 staff members from housekeeping and engineering. A large and complex convention had been held the first week of the following quarter. He had to pay the additional staff $6.50/hr., and he had needed 15 of them for two days of eight hours' work. All the work had been done in the quarter under question, but the convention itself wasn't held until the next quarter — Dave felt that he was being unjustly penalized because of the timing.

THE MEETING

The General Manager reviewed both Admiral's Hotel's balance sheet (Figure 4) and the specific numbers for the Functions Department (Figure 1). But his meeting with Mike proved to be counter productive. Mike refused to take responsibility for the Functions Department's loss. He said that since he could not make decisions to control the Department, he should not be held accountable for it. But the General Manager pointed out that someone had to be responsible.

Dave's meeting with the General Manager was not much better. Dave recounted his grievances. He pointed out that his Department was assigned costs over which it has no control. The General Manager responded that all the other Divisions/Department have the same allocation procedure. As well, it had always been done that way.

CASE REQUIREMENT

In an effort to resolve the problem, the General Manager contacted an outside accountant who specialized in management accounting; his study turned up some further facts. Assume the role of the outside accountant, and outline your assessment of the Functions Department's fourth quarter results.

ENDNOTE

[1] *The monthly hours were calculated at 30 days at 8 hours per day, for all budget and actual amounts. Please use these figures.*

FIGURE 1
ADMIRAL'S HOTEL — PART (B)
FUNCTIONS DEPARTMENT
4th quarter ended April 30, 1987 (in dollars)

Revenue	Actual	Budget
Food	197,500	200,000
Liquor	270,000	250,000
Room Rental	60,000	55,000
Total Revenue	527,500	505,000
Expenses [1]		
Cost of Sales – Food	71,275	72,000
Cost of Sales – Liquor	82,950	77,500
Labour	145,200	129,600
Supplies	21,000	18,000
Administration	174,275	157,500
Total Expenses	494,700	454,600
Net Revenue	32,800	50,400

Note

[1] *All costs are variable, except Administration, which is a non-discretionary, fixed cost. Do not reestablish behaviour, but accept the behaviour as here noted.*

FIGURE 2
ADMIRAL'S HOTEL — PART (B)
BONUS STRUCTURE

BONUS SYSTEM

The company has a varied ROI based on department and on which quarter of the year. A summary is as follows:

	1st	2nd	3rd	4th
Rooms	4%	5%	5%	2%
Restaurant	0%	1%	1%	0%
Lounge	1%	1%	2%	1%
Pub	2%	2%	2%	1%

Total Hotel Annual ROI = 30%

The Functions Department operates under the Rooms Division, and has been allocated ROI's of:

	.9	.9	1.5	0.75

The Investment base includes Working Capital plus all other assets.

The bonus system is as follows:

LOWER TIER

1% of annual salary if the manager's ROI exceeds the required ROI by between 10% and 25%.

HIGHER TIER

If the manager's ROI exceeds the required ROI by 25% or more, the bonus is the ROI times the quarter's salary.

FOR EXAMPLE

Rooms Division 1st quarter ROI is 4%.

If ROI is 5% (that is 4% + 25% of 4%), bonus is 1% of salary.

If ROI is 6% (that is 4% + 50% of 4%), bonus is 6% of quarterly salary.

FIGURE 3
ADMIRAL'S HOTEL — PART (B)

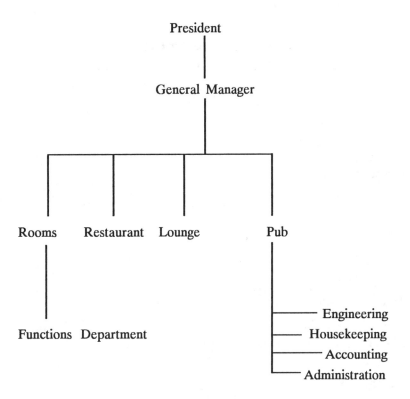

FIGURE 4
ADMIRAL'S HOTEL — PART (B)
BALANCE SHEET (in dollars)
(Unaudited, Unadjusted)
April 30, 1987

Assets

Current Assets

Cash	2,000
Accounts Receivable	250,000
Temporary Investments	25,000
Inventory	100,000
Prepaid Expenses	1,000
Total Current Assets	378,000

Fixed Assets

Land	822,000
Building	3,250,000
Equipment	1,700,000
Total Fixed Assets	5,772,000
Total Assets	6,150,000

Liabilities and Shareholders' Equity

Current Liabilities

Accounts Payable	175,000
Long-Term Debt	4,074,000
Total Liabilities	4,249,000

Shareholders' Equity

Share Capital	1,000,000
Retained Earnings	901,000
Total Shareholders' Equity	1,901,000
Total Liabilities and Shareholders' Equity	6,150,000

CASE 4

FRANK'S LOCKER SERVICE (1984) INC.

M. Fine
Lakehead University
Thunder Bay, Ontario

J. Thatcher
Lakehead University
Thunder Bay, Ontario

Mike Petrone, owner of Frank's Locker Service in Thunder Bay, Ontario, sat in his office one February day in 1986 examining his accounts. A significant portion of his business was the purchasing of A1 beef, the butchering of it, and the selling of the various cuts. He knew the cost of the beef, but he was not sure how to calculate the cost of the butchering process.

COMPANY HISTORY

Frank Petrone, Mike's father, had founded the business in the early 1950's. Originally, the business focused on butchering and selling quality meats, providing cold storage service, and renting freezer locker space to consumers; however, home freezers became more popular in the 1960's and the need for freezer lockers declined. Starting in the late 1950's, the opening of the St. Lawrence Seaway had increased ship traffic to its western terminus, the port of Thunder Bay. These ships needed meats, groceries, and other sundry items delivered to dockside while cargoes were being loaded during the April to December shipping season. This was an opportunity for Frank to increase his business. Frank's Locker Service entered the market and became the leading ship chandler for the port.

As a ship chandler, Frank's Locker Service augmented its inventory to include not only meat, but a variety of groceries, produce and sundry items. When a ship came into port, the ship's cook contacted Frank's to order supplies. If an item was out of stock or if a hardware item was required, Frank's arranged to get the item to the ship. The major function of the business became ship chandlery.

Goods to provide this service were acquired in various ways. Grocery items were bought in bulk if price incentives and storage room were available. Out-of-stock items and produce could be obtained on short notice from local wholesalers. Meat items were purchased in several ways and required varying amounts of processing. Whole chickens and turkeys were purchased in carload quantities, stored in freezers, and sold without processing. Chicken parts were ordered in bulk and divided into smaller packages, but no cutting was required. Beef and pork, on the other hand, did require processing. These meats were purchased by the carcass and butchered into standard cuts. Scraps and less desirable cuts were processed into sausages, cold cuts, and smoked meats.

Ship chandlery continued to be the mainstay of the business throughout the 1970's. During the 1980's, however, cargo volumes and the number of ships through the port began to decline. This was the result of a number of factors: alternate western grain ports opened, grain harvests diminished, export sales of Canadian grain declined, and larger ships were built. To make matters worse for ship chandlery in Thunder Bay, modern ships employed fewer crew members and had better food storage facilities on board. Thus, many ships purchased enough food in eastern ports to make a round trip and required fewer provisions in Thunder Bay.

In 1984, after having worked for his father for ten years, Mike purchased the business. He was an expert meat cutter; he had supervised the delivery, shipping and receiving activities; and he had managed the business for short periods during his father's vacations. However, as the new owner, Mike took on two new responsibilities — buying and price setting — with which he had little previous experience.

Mike understood that the shipping business was still the major trade, but he needed to cultivate new markets in order to ensure his future. One market opportunity already existed: local hospitals and geriatric care facilities requested bids on meat orders each week. The bidding process was open to any supplier, and bids were accepted on an item-by-item basis. For example, if the institution asked for bids on four items, the lowest bid on each item would be accepted. Because of the item-by-item basis, if any supplier won by bidding below cost for one item there was no guarantee that he would be able to compensate for the loss with a profit on another item. Mike decided to compete in this market, and as this segment of his business grew in volume from 1984 to 1986, he realized that it was critical to have a comprehensive understanding of the business's cost structure.

BEEF COSTS AND VOLUMES

The company's accounting records consisted of a cash receipts journal, a cash disbursements journal, a general ledger and an accounts receivable sub-ledger. Purchase invoices were filed by supplier and sales invoices were filed by customer name. In the general ledger, neither sales nor purchases were segregated by product line; this made it impossible to calculate the gross margin on meat sales. Payroll information disclosed gross pay and hours worked, but it was impossible to identify the number of hours spent on cutting beef.

Even though no formal information was available, Mike summarized total meat-cutter labour hours and costs for 1985 (see Exhibit 1). Next he used the supplier invoices to determine the volume and cost of meat purchased during the year (see Exhibit 2). He estimated the time required to perform each butchering task, and applied the estimated time to the volume of meat purchased. For example, he knew it took approximately 2.5 hours to butcher a side of A1 beef. The supplier invoices revealed that 207 sides had been purchased. The estimated total hours spent in 1985 to butcher 207 sides is derived by multiplying 2.5 hours by 207 sides, resulting in an estimated 517.5 hours on sides of A1 beef. This process provided the basis for the hours directly traceable to butchering, and Mike felt that these estimates were reasonable.

Mike selected information reported in the 1985 financial statements that he thought might be important in determining the true cost of each cut of A1 beef (see Exhibit 3). He was certain that wrapping supplies, repairs to the meat-cutting equipment, meat-cutter coffee and clean-up time, and freight-in were 100 percent attributable to total meat costs. He felt that roughly one half of the delivery floor labour, repairs to refrigeration equipment and equipment depreciation should be assigned to total meat costs. Mike was uncertain whether to include any portion of the other business costs in his calculation.

Industry standards were available for consumer cuts of beef. Mike adjusted these standards to reflect the products which he produced for the shipping trade and local institutional requirements (see Exhibit 4). The Waste Adjustment Factor identified the true cost of a kilogram of each cut after an allowance for waste. For example, the cost of a rump roast cut from a side of A1 beef was determined by multiplying the cost per kilogram of a side by the Waste Adjustment Factor of 1.61. However, if the same rump roast was cut from a hind of beef the Waste Adjustment Factor was 1.30. This reflected the greater waste associated with the side. The weighted average cost per kilogram was calculated from supplier invoices for 1985. As expected, the cost of hinds always exceeded the cost of sides.

As Mike turned over the pages of the account journals, he wondered where he should begin and how he was going to determine his prices based on his desired gross margin of 20 percent. He wanted to have a firm pricing policy in place before the busy season started in April.

EXHIBIT 1
FRANK'S LOCKER SERVICE (1984) INC.
MEAT-CUTTER LABOUR HOURS – 1985

Traceable Direct Hours	Estimated Hours
Sides of Beef, Grade A1	517.5
Hinds of Beef, Grade A1	200.7
Longloins, Grade A1	81.5
Shortloins, Grade A1	59.0
Sides of Beef, Grade C1	668.1
Pork Shoulders, Butts and Loins	99.0
Pork Bellies	212.2
Fresh Hams	456.8
Sausages, Cold Cuts, etc.	650.0
Miscellaneous Cutting	323.7
Traceable Direct Hours	3,268.5

Other Hours

Clean-Up (Approx. 5 Hours/Week)	250.0
Coffee Breaks	250.0
Total Other Hours	500.0
Total Meat-Cutter Hours 1985	3,768.5

MEAT-CUTTER COSTS – 1985
(in dollars)

Butcher	Amount Paid*	Hours Worked
Head Butcher	21,602	1,858.0
Apprentice	16,567	1,910.5
	38,169	3,768.5

*Amount paid includes vacation pay, Worker's Compensation premiums, and the employer portion of UIC and CPP contributions for the head butcher and apprentice.

Note

No allocation of Mike Petrone's wages at $14.50 per hour was included in these costs. Occasionally, during the busy season, he assisted the butchers.

EXHIBIT 2
FRANK'S LOCKER SERVICE (1984) INC.
SCHEDULE OF VOLUMES AND COSTS
FOR MEAT PURCHASES – 1985 (in dollars)

"Accurate"

Item	Volume kg	Units	Cost
Sides of Beef, Grade A1*	26,243	207	79,202
Hinds of Beef, Grade A1*	11,695	172	43,776
Longloins Beef, Grade A1*	3,843	168	19,705
Shortloins Beef, Grade A1*	2,128	236	12,610
Sides of Beef, Grade C1*	40,944		99,331
Beef Heart, Liver, etc.	9,504		12,373
Side of Pork*	951		2,143
Pork Butts*	7,604		17,420
Pork Shoulder*	2,217		4,967
Spareribs	6,137		10,501
Pork Loins*	8,332		24,816
Pork Side Ribs	705		2,161
Bacon (Ready To Go)	3,701		9,923
Pork Jowls	1,871		2,062
Pork Hocks	1,200		1,187
Pork Bellies*	9,278		18,051
Hams (Ready To Go)	3,503		14,882
Fresh Hams (Pork Legs)*	37,046		74,438
Pork Tenderloin	275		1,792
Sausage (Ready To Go)	230		626
Chicken Breasts	2,300		7,653
Chicken Legs and 9 Cut	2,329		4,934
Grade A Chickens, Whole	983		2,984
Utility Grade Chickens	9,843		20,080
Turkeys, Grade A	14,074		39,637
Turkeys, Utility Grade	19,687		53,931
Corn Beef (Ready To Go)	596		1,370
Bologna and Wieners	6,368		9,245
Fish and Seafood	6,160		15,416

*These purchases require butchering.

EXHIBIT 3
FRANK'S LOCKER SERVICE (1984) INC.
SUMMARY SCHEDULE OF COSTS — 1985 (in dollars)

Description	Amount
Wholly Attributable to Meats	
Wrapping Supplies	3,181
Repairs & Maintenance (Meat Cutting Equipment)	3,009
Meat Cutter Coffee & Clean-Up Time	5,065
Freight-In (Fish & Chicken Only)	11,621
Total	22,876
Partially Attributable to Meats	
Delivery Floor Labour	20,974
Repairs to Refrigeration Equipment	6,000
Equipment Depreciation	9,996
Total	36,970
Other Business Costs	
Delivery Costs	
Insurance	5,490
Depreciation	6,871
Gas, Oil, Repairs	11,862
Occupancy Costs	
Building Insurance	9,899
Property Taxes	15,386
Rent	16,660
Utilities	24,659
Salaries (Office and Management)	47,394
Miscellaneous	6,761
Total	144,982

CASE 4 39

pg 304-305

EXHIBIT 4
FRANK'S LOCKER SERVICE (1984) INC.
WASTE ADJUSTMENT FACTORS FOR A1 BEEF

Item	1985 Weighted Average $/kg	Waste Factor Adjustment	
Sides of Beef	3.02	1.00	~126.78 kg/unit
Boneless Round Steak	$7.34	1.61	
Rump Roast	7.34	1.61	
Sirloin Tip	8.07	1.77	
Sirloin Steak	8.25	1.81	
T-Bone Steak	8.25	1.81	
Rib Roast	5.88	1.29	
Flank Steak	4.70	1.03	
Braising Ribs	3.33	0.73	
Blade Roast (Bone out)	5.11	1.12	
Corned Beef	6.79	1.49	
Stew Beef	5.43	1.19	
Hamburger	4.20	0.92	
Hinds	3.74	1.00	67.99 kg/unit
Boneless Round Steak	$7.06	1.30	
Rump Roast	7.06	1.30	
Sirloin Tip	7.76	1.43	
Sirloin Steak	7.93	1.46	
T-Bone Steak	7.93	1.46	
Flank Steak	4.51	0.83	
Longloins	5.16	1.00	22.875 kg/unit
Sirloin Steak	7.25	1.00	
T-Bone Steak	7.25	1.00	
Shortloins	5.93	1.00	
T-Bone Steak	$8.30	1.00	9.02 kg/unit

CASE 5

ARRISCRAFT CORPORATION

H. Teall
Wilfrid Laurier University
Waterloo, Ontario

In February 1988, Randy White, President of Arriscraft Corporation, had just received requests for prices on two of its marble products. The first request was from a nearby city for 140,000 square feet, or approximately 2,000 tonnes, of paving stones. The second request was from a construction firm in Ohio, which requested a price on 3,000 tonnes of window sills of varying sizes. While White was confident that a price of $300 a tonne for the paving stones and $500 a tonne for the window sills would result in Arriscraft receiving the orders, he was unsure that these prices would result in a reasonable profit.

COMPANY BACKGROUND

Arriscraft had been established in Cambridge, Ontario, in 1949 by E.B. Ratcliffe, a chemical engineer, to produce precast stones. In 1956 he developed a unique process which compressed sand into stone without the use of cement. The result was a stone which was more durable than the normal clay bricks or other masonry products and which could be formed into a variety of shapes, sizes, colours and textures.

In 1962 Arriscraft added a second product line which involved the cutting of limestone blocks from a quarry near Wiarton, Ontario and the production of marble hearth slabs and window sills in Cambridge. In 1980 additional marble products, of paving stones and building stones, were added to the line. These marble products were sold under the trade name of Adair Marble.

As of 1988 the company was the only producer of the manufactured stones in the world and was Canada's largest producer of marble products, with only one smaller competitor located in Winnipeg, Manitoba. Recently Arriscraft had been successful in obtaining some significant contracts which included supplying the marble stone for the Canadian Chancery in Washington, the Ontario Court House and

Registry Office in Ottawa, and the reconstruction of the Rideau Canal locks. With these and other contracts, Arriscraft had established a reputation among architects and contractors as a leading producer of unique and top quality stone products.

White had been with the company for nine years, after graduating from Queen's University with a degree in commerce and obtaining his Chartered Accountant's designation. During his nine years, White held the positions of Controller, Executive Vice-President and President. With this experience he was fully aware of both the financial and the technical implications of the various alternatives that he faced. In particular, he was acutely aware that the variability of the yields and product mix significantly complicated any analysis of product line profitability.

PRODUCTION PROCESS

As the decisions facing White concerned marble products, only the production process related to these products will be described. Exhibit 1 illustrates the following description of the process.

First, limestone blocks are drilled and cut from a quarry. The top surface of the quarry is the side of the block, the dimensions being 30 inches by 84 inches. The depth of the block will vary depending upon the natural bed depth of the quarry, but lengths vary from 3 feet to 10 feet. The net results are limestone blocks which vary in size from 4 to 12 metric tonnes, with an average size being approximately 8 tonnes. These limestone blocks are then trucked to Arriscraft's plant. The total direct costs of the limestone blocks are approximately $50 per tonne, which includes the removal and transportation costs.

At the plant, each limestone block is positioned in front of a saw which first cuts off two sides. These cuts will remove approximately 1 tonne of waste from an average 8 tonne block, leaving 7 tonnes. Next the saw operator must make a series of critical judgment calls as the operator proceeds to cut the limestone block into slices called product blocks. The saw operator must examine the face of the stone for cracks, pits or other faults. If any are found, a cut approximately 8 inches wide will be made and the product block will be further processed into paving stones. If the limestone block is reasonably clear of faults, then a 6 inch cut will be made and the product block will be processed into window sills. If the stone is of highest quality then cuts varying from 6 to 30 inches will be made to produce specialized products and hearth slabs. A fourth product line is referred to as larger units, where the quality may be low, and these sections would otherwise be used for paving stones. However, if a wider cut is made, the stone can be used in place of some top quality large pieces for some specific applications. The skill of the saw operator is extremely important as a limestone block will normally produce many grades of products, and thus a judgment call is required after each cut is made. The cutting of the limestone block into product blocks results in an 80% yield of the 7 tonnes, and the cutting costs per tonne of product block vary for each of the four product lines as follows:

Paving stones	$14 per tonne
Window sills	$15 per tonne
Hearth slabs	$10 per tonne
Large units	$12 per tonne

While a variance of 10 to 15% exists, it is expected that 10% of the product block tonnage will be in paving stones, 40% in window sills, 40% in hearth slabs, and 10% in large units.

The processing of the product blocks into their designated final products first involves some additional sawing and splitting. Then depending upon the quality of the final product, the stones are honed (smoothed) to produce the marble product.

The extent of the processing varies by product line, and the ultimate yield will also vary by product line. The paving stones have a 50% yield and the processing costs total $115 per tonne of finished product. The window sills have a yield of 48% with a processing cost of $180 per tonne of finished product. The waste from the window sills can be used for paving stones, and after a further processing cost of $65 per tonne of finished product, a yield of 21% of the waste is obtained. The hearth slabs are processed for a cost of $150 per tonne of finished product and a 65% yield of the product blocks. The large units result in a yield of 70% with a processing cost of $75 per finished tonne. The above is the typical production process; however, it is also possible to produce paving stones and window sills from higher grade material. While the cutting and processing costs for the paving stones and window sills would remain the same, the yields would increase as follows. Window sills may be cut from the material that would normally be used for hearth slabs and large units and the yields would increase by 10 percentage points to 75% and 80% respectively. Similarly, paving stones may be cut from window sill, hearth slab, and large unit materials with a 15 percentage point increase in yields to 63%, 80% and 85% respectively. In addition, the cutting of paving stones from window sill waste would increase to 31%. White was, however, concerned that this alternate production process would not yield satisfactory profit margins.

SITUATION SUMMARY

White had been faced many times with similar situations to the one before him. If 2,000 tonnes of paving stones were produced by means of the normal production process, more than the required quantities of window sills must also be produced. Furthermore, product blocks that would eventually be processed into hearth slabs and large units must also be cut even though they were not currently required. However, if the limestone blocks were cut into only paving stones, only window sills, or both paving stones and window sills, the higher quality material would be used where lower quality material would meet the customer requirements.

The market for these marble products was somewhat unpredictable, as the orders tended to be large and depended essentially upon the preferences of an architect or contractor. While Arriscraft did not have any direct competition, it did have competition from less expensive alternative building products. For example, the paving stones would cost the city $4.29 a square foot, whereas interlocking brick (an alternative cement-based product) would cost $1 to $2 a square foot. Essentially the issue was how much more the market would be willing to pay for a marble product than for a more common alternative.

Given the common costs of the limestone block and the cutting, White again wondered whether a price of $300 per tonne of paving stones and $500 per tonne of window sills would generate sufficient profits. As a rule of thumb, the company had historically attempted to attain a mark-up of 100% on the direct product costs. Typically, a mark-up of less than 70% was viewed as unprofitable. However, in a situation such as this, the measurement of the direct costs by product line was not straightforward. Furthermore, the unsold product, both finished and unfinished, had always presented a problem when costing the inventory for Arriscraft's annual financial report. Depending upon the approach adopted, the costing of the inventory could have a material effect on the net income of Arriscraft Corporation.

EXHIBIT 1
ARRISCRAFT CORPORATION
TYPICAL PRODUCTION PROCESS FOR MARBLE PRODUCTS

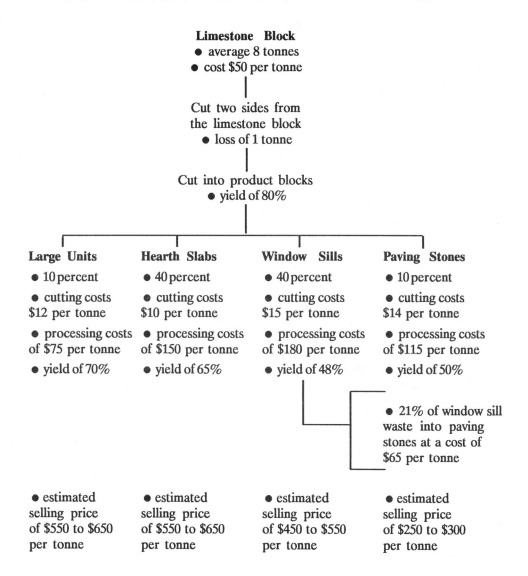

CASE 6

QUALITY DESIGN AND PRINT LIMITED

W. Murphy
University College
of Cape Breton
Sydney, Nova Scotia

S. MacKenzie
University College
of Cape Breton
Sydney, Nova Scotia

THE FIRM

Quality Design and Print Ltd. is a small design and print shop located in Lawrencetown, British Columbia. The company's capital stock is owned entirely by Keith MacKay, who purchased the struggling two-year old firm in 1982 and brought it back from the brink of bankruptcy. The firm has steadily increased in sales since that time, but profits have not always kept pace.

Quality Design employs nine full-time staff. The present manager is Mark Johnson, who holds a degree in Business Administration. Johnson was originally hired as a sales agent, but his role quickly changed to that of assistant manager. In the summer of 1987 he was promoted to manager, when Keith MacKay left that position to devote more time to a new business venture in consulting and communications.

MacKay saw this new business as a complement to the print shop. He felt that through development of programs (advertising, communications, etc.) for different businesses, Quality Design and Print would be able to profit from the spin-off printing work which would result. MacKay also felt that through this new venture contacts could be made to help widen Quality Design's printing market. At present theconsulting business is not separate from the printing business, and all revenues from current work are recorded as consulting revenues for the company.

THE MARKET

Lawrencetown is a small city with a population of approximately 35,000. Quality Design and Print Ltd. services Lawrencetown and the surrounding area, a total population of 70,000.

The company has four main competitors. The oldest and largest of these is the Lawrencetown Printing Company. It has been in operation for about twenty years and had total sales of approximately $1 million in 1986. White Printers is the next largest competitor with sales of about $350,000; a third competitor, Linear Printing Services, has sales of some $200,000. Both White and Linear Printing are well established firms that have been operating for over fifteen years. The newest competitor, a franchise operation which has been in business for two years, has sales estimated at $150,000. The sales figures for Quality Design and Print appear in Exhibits 1 and 2.

The market is very competitive and usually all five firms will bid on the same job. Lawrencetown Printers has an advantage on certain colour work as its equipment is more advanced, while the other firms must contract out these orders.

Quality's new manager, Mark Johnson, feels that the firm is presently operating at less than 75% capacity. However, there are no figures to support his conclusion. The firm does not record machine production time (along with offsetting down-time) nor does it formally budget production hours. Johnson also believes that Quality Design should not be too aggressive in its marketing approach. He feels that they should gradually develop a solid client foundation based on a reputation for excellent work.

PRODUCTS

Quality Design and Print produces a wide variety of products including stationery, brochures, tickets, NCR forms, posters, booklets and pamphlets. The firm's services include laminating, design, layouts, typesetting and, the main source of revenue, printing.

Printing is divided into two categories: quality print and quick print. Quality print uses a metal plate to produce an image and provides the customer with a high quality product; the plate can be stored for future use. Quick print uses a significantly cheaper paper plate to produce the image and provides a less expensive, lower quality product; the paper plate has a very limited life.

PRICING POLICY

Quality Design prices its jobs using a job cost sheet (see Exhibit 3). This sheet breaks down costs into two major categories. The first is direct material costs: including the number of pages, type of paper required, type of ink required, and binding procedures.

The direct materials are recorded on the sheet at cost. Folding and binding also require an application of a cost rate. The number of sheets to be folded, for example, is multiplied by an established rate. This rate covers the direct labour cost involved in performing this aspect of the job. To cover overhead and profit, a 40% mark-up is then applied to these costs. Johnson feels that approximately 15% of this mark-up will result in profit.

It should be noted that the firm does not apply any of its overhead to jobs. Total overhead is not budgeted and no overhead rates exist. Instead, the 40% mark-up is believed to be sufficient to cover the firm's overhead in all cases. Quality Design also applies a 10% waste factor to larger jobs. This percentage is applied to paper cost only and occurs before the 40% standard mark-up.

The other major costs category involves production department expenses. These relate to the number of hours required to perform certain tasks related to a job. The number of hours estimated on the costing sheet are multiplied by established rates to arrive at the total estimated production costs. Again, no overhead is applied and a 40% mark-up is used.

QUOTATION

The sum of the production department costs and the direct material costs is the price quotation.

As the job progresses, the actual hours and materials required are recorded on a production envelope (see Exhibit 4). The envelope is used to compare actual costs to estimated costs. In situations where the firm gives estimated quotations, if the actual costs exceed the estimated, then the price will be increased if the difference is material, although it may not be increased (even if material) if the customer is an important source of business. If the estimated costs exceed actual, the firm will usually bill for the estimated price unless the difference is substantial, in which case they will reduce the billing price by an appropriate amount.

PRICING DIFFICULTIES

Mark Johnson had been working at the firm for a year and a half when he became manager. Johnson believes that the current job costing procedure is adequate. He has stated that, "You develop a *feel* for costing in the printing business, and over time your ability to cost accurately improves." Pricing a job is difficult because usually all the printing firms will be competing for the same job, and the shop with the lowest bid most often wins. Johnson commented, "I might spend two hours costing a job and we wind up losing the bid. There goes two hours of my time which might have been used more productively." It should be pointed out that Johnson does not factor his time spent on costing a job into the eventual price quotation. For a flow of information related to the costing process, refer to Exhibit 5.

JOB FLOW

The receptionist takes a customer call. The request for a job is passed on to the manager, who develops a price quote using the pricing methods previously described. The manager then calls the customer with the firm's price and, if the customer accepts, Johnson sends the job to the Art Department for initial design (if design is required). The Art Department sends the designed job (proof) back to the manager who shows it to the customer. If changes are recommended, then it goes back to the Art Department. From here, the job goes to the Print Shop for printing. After the printing process is completed, Johnson is notified. He compares actual costs to budgeted costs and then informs the customer that the job is completed and ready to be picked up. In the event that Johnson is unavailable, the bookkeeper or owner (if present) will fill in.

COSTS

Mark Johnson believes that the costs for Quality Design and Print Ltd. are, for the most part, variable. He also finds that expenses are rising at a faster rate than sales. However, there are no cost–cutting procedures taking place, and prices cannot be greatly increased due to the competitive nature of the business. Exhibit 6 contains a breakdown of the firm's employee positions and corresponding labour rates.

ACCOUNTING SYSTEM

The accounting system at Quality Design and Print is designed mainly for tax purposes. Accounting data (entries) are collected and recorded manually by the bookkeeper, Bernice Gillis. She holds a Bachelor of Business Administration degree and has been working with the firm for four years. Gillis records all cash inflows and outflows, prepares the cheques, and co-signs cheques with the manager. She provides monthly posting summaries to an outside accountant. The financial statements are prepared on a quarterly basis and given to the owner, Keith MacKay. Mark Johnson does not have access to the financial statements.

The financial statements are not used for budgeting purposes. In fact, there has never been a budget drawn up even though Johnson feels it would be a good idea. He finds that he is just too busy to have the time to construct any kind of budget.

CREDIT POLICY

The firm's credit policy is Net 30 with a 2% interest charge per month on outstanding balances. Johnson says that the firm does not pursue collection of interest on overdue accounts, nor have they considered giving discounts for early payment. But he feels that something should be done about overdue accounts, considering that 85% of the firm's sales are on credit.

PURCHASES

The firm has two main suppliers offering terms of 2/10 Net 30 and 2/15 Net 30 on all direct material purchases. Quality does not take advantage of the discounts as it feels that adequate cash levels must be maintained throughout the year (note that no cash budgeting procedures are in place). Quality Design prefers to let their payables accumulate through the year and to clean up their balance sheet by payment in January and February before the year end (February 28).

CONCLUDING COMMENTS

In late February, 1988, Keith MacKay was heading to Central Canada to purchase a printing machine with a larger paper size capacity. He was also looking at purchasing a larger folding machine. He hopes that these additions will do four things: (1) increase sales, (2) lower operating expenses, (3) save time, and (4) provide an edge over the competition. No cost-benefit analysis was undertaken to arrive at the decision to purchase these pieces of equipment.

Upon his return, MacKay plans to direct his attention to the development and breakaway of the consulting venture. However, concerns about financial planning and budgeting are quite serious and must also be addressed. In addition, the system of accountability for the manager of the printing business must be considered.

EXHIBIT 1
QUALITY DESIGN AND PRINT LIMITED
INCOME STATEMENT (in dollars)
(Unaudited)
For the Years Ended February 28, 1987, 1986, and 1985

	1987	1986	1985
Sales	274,145	252,329	219,497
Cost of Sales			
Beginning Inventory	5,716	5,086	3,826
Purchases, Including Outside Services	81,115	69,928	63,413
Freight In	376	439	796
	87,207	75,453	68,035
Ending Inventory	3,993	5,716	5,086
	83,214	69,737	62,949
Gross Profit	190,931	182,592	156,548
Expenses			
Salaries, Wages & Benefits	128,096	124,834	98,954
Rent	10,400	10,600	10,400
Bad Debts	11,122	8,644	-0-
Depreciation	9,499	7,204	1,641
Telephone	5,026	4,999	4,922
Office Expense	4,448	6,578	5,806
Equipment Rental	2,545	3,382	25,200
Interest and Bank Charges	3,391	4,668	669
Occupancy Tax	1,947	1,494	1,391
Power	3,824	-0-	890
Professional Fees	3,195	2,455	1,306
Travel and Promotion	3,721	4,309	2,697
Insurance	345	345	-0-
Membership	125	1,053	-0-
Miscellaneous	2,575	2,044	3,819
Total Expenses	190,259	182,609	157,695
Operating Income	672	(17)	(1,147)
Other Income	1,639	1,322	6,735
Income Before Extraordinary Item	2,311	1,305	5,588
Extraordinary Item	-0-	47,400	-0-
Net Income	2,311	48,705	5,588

EXHIBIT 1a
QUALITY DESIGN AND PRINT LIMITED
INCOME STATEMENT (in dollars)
(Unaudited)
For the nine months ended November 30

	1987	1986
Sales	245,838	222,961
Cost of Sales		
Beginning Inventory	3,993	5,716
Purchases, Including outside services	83,899	67,838
Freight In	264	319
Goods Available for Sale	88,156	73,873
Ending inventory	4,781	5,354
Cost of Sales	83,375	68,519
Gross Profit	162,463	154,442
Expenses		
Salaries, Wages and Benefits	114,572	101,691
Rent	7,800	7,800
Telephone	4,520	3,649
Office Expenses	4,693	3,111
Power	2,401	2,630
Van Expense	868	2,513
Copier	1,569	2,248
Professional Fees	420	1,723
Loan Interest	2,107	1,575
Occupancy Tax	979	995
Travel and Promotion	1,722	1,385
Interest and Bank Charges	335	234
Advertising	1,166	301
Membership and Dues	125	125
Miscellaneous	3,306	1,822
Depreciation	7,651	9,381
Repairs	1,280	-0-
Xerox Rental	515	-0-
Total Expenses	156,029	141,183
Operating Income	6,434	13,259
Other Income	4,076	-0-
	10,510	13,259
Provision for Income Taxes	2,700	3,400
Net Income for the Period	7,810	9,859

EXHIBIT 2
QUALITY DESIGN AND PRINT LIMITED
BALANCE SHEET (in dollars)
(Unaudited)
As at February 28

ASSETS	1987	1986	1985
Current			
Cash	4,429	11,213	2,088
Accounts Receivable			
Trade	40,950	44,119	32,330
Other	54	-0-	5,000
Employees	-0-	-0-	1,002
Inventory	3,993	5,716	5,086
Total Current Assets	49,426	61,048	45,506
Fixed — At Cost			
Equipment	74,521	72,038	19,217
Van	11,237	-0-	-0-
	85,758	72,038	19,217
Less Accumulated Depreciation	18,254	8,844	1,641
Total Fixed Assets	67,504	63,194	17,576
Organization Expense At Cost	1,040	1,040	1,040
Total Assets	117,970	125,282	64,122
LIABILITIES AND EQUITY			
Current			
Accounts Payable	7,075	5,628	10,245
Accrued Liabilities	27,365	38,420	72,388
Current Portion of Long-term Debt	11,875	10,000	-0-
Total Current Liabilities	46,315	54,048	82,633
Long-Term Debt			
Note — Bank of Nova Scotia	8,110	-0-	-0-
Mortgage Payable	15,000	25,000	15,000
Total Long-Term Debt	23,110	25,000	15,000
Total Liabilities	69,425	79,048	97,633
Equity			
Shareholder's Loan	30,000	30,000	-0-
Capital Stock	3	3	3
Contributed Surplus	4,040	4,040	3,000
Retained Earnings	14,502	12,191	(36,514)
Total Equity	48,545	46,234	(33,511)
Total Liabilities & Equity	117,970	125,282	64,122

EXHIBIT 2a
QUALITY DESIGN AND PRINT LIMITED
BALANCE SHEET (in dollars)
(Unaudited)
As at November 30

	1987	1986
ASSETS		
Current		
Cash	3,494	13,415
Accounts Receivable — Trade	67,864	47,147
— Other	154	-0-
Inventory	4,781	5,354
Total Current Assets	76,293	65,916
Fixed — At Cost		
Equipment	75,596	72,621
Van	11,237	11,237
	86,833	83,858
Less Accumulated Depreciation	25,995	19,141
Total Fixed Assets	60,838	64,717
Organization Expense — At Cost	1,040	1,040
Total Assets	138,171	131,673
LIABILITIES AND EQUITY		
Current		
Accounts Payable and Accruals	38,254	29,817
Sales Taxes Payable	5,774	3,061
Income Taxes Payable	2,700	3,400
Current Portion of Long-Term Debt	12,000	11,560
Total Current Liabilities	58,728	47,838
Long-Term Debt		
Bank Loan — Van	6,604	8,617
Mortgage Payable	13,500	17,500
Total Long-Term Debt	20,104	26,117
Total Liabilities	78,832	73,955
Equity		
Shareholder's Loan	30,000	30,000
Capital Stock	3	3
Contributed Surplus	4,040	4,040
Retained Earnings	25,296	23,675
Total Equity	59,339	57,718
Total Liabilities & Equity	138,171	131,673

© John Wiley & Sons Canada Ltd. All rights reserved.

EXHIBIT 3

QUOTATION REQUEST

Date required: ___/d ___/m ___/y

Client _____ Products: _____

Address _____ Quantity: (1)____ (2)____ (3)____

_____ Art Dept.: _____

_____ Printer: _____

Telephone _____ Outside Service: _____

Contact _____ Date in_____ Due date_____

PRODUCTION DEPARTMENT
Description: _____
_____
_____

PRINT SHOP
☐ Quality Print   ☐ Quick Print
Products: _____ Ink _____
No. of pgs ____ 1☐ 2☐ sides

Required	Hrs.	Total
☐ proofreading	___	___
☐ layout	___	___
☐ artwork	___	___
☐ colour separation	___	___
☐ presentation	___	___
☐ paste up	___	___
☐ typesetting	___	___
☐ copy	___	___
☐ consulting	___	___

Stock _____ D/M _____
Wt. _____ Sz. _____ Colour _____
Trim size _____
No. up _____ Run size _____ No. out _____
Full sheets required?   yes ☐ no ☐
Bleed ____ sides
Stock _____
Wt. _____ Sz. _____ Colour _____
Trim size _____
Full sheets required?   yes ☐ no ☐
Bleed ____ sides

Camera	No.	Total
☐ positives	___	___
☐ reverse	___	___
☐ screens	___	___
☐ transparencies	___	___

☐ Fold _____ places   Plastic bind _____
☐ Perf _____ places (colour)
☐ Score _____ places   Size _____
☐ Collate _____   Bundles of _____
Number ___ places   Drill _____ places
_____ to _____   ☐ Perfect bind pkg.
☐ Stitch _____ places ☐ Wrap
☐ Trim _____ sides   ☐ Laminate
☐ Pad books of _____   ☐ Round corners
☐ Pad NCR
Notes:

OUTSIDE SERVICES
Company _____
Address _____
Telephone _____
Contact _____
Quote _____
Shipped via _____
Notes:

Set-up _____
Qty   (1) _____
      (2) _____
      (3) _____
Total _____

EXHIBIT 4
PRODUCTION ENVELOPE

Client _____
Address _____
Postal Code _____ Telephone _____ Contact _____
Product _____
___ Art Dept. _____ Printer _____ Outside Service _____
Date in _____ Delivery Date _____ Time _____
Proof Date _____ Time _____
Job# _____ Reorder _____ Previous Job # _____
Purchase order # _____ Order taken by _____

PRODUCTION DEPARTMENT

Required	Finished	Hours	Total
☐ Proofreading	_____	_____	_____
☐ Lay-out	_____	_____	_____
☐ Artwork	_____	_____	_____
☐ Colour Separations	_____	_____	_____
☐ Presentation	_____	_____	_____
☐ Paste Up	_____	_____	_____
☐ Typesetting	_____	_____	_____

Camera		No.	Total
☐ Positives		_____	_____
☐ Reverses		_____	_____
☐ Transparencies		_____	_____
☐ Screens		_____	_____

Notes _____

Newspaper/Magazine ☐ B & W ☐ Colour
Publication _____ Column Width _____ picas
Ad Size _____ Col X _____ lines
Half tones __65% __85% __100% __133% TOTAL _____
Notes _____

(1)

PRINTING
                                        Press
Products _____ Qty _____ No. Pgs. _____ 1 Side ☐ 2 Sides ☐
A _____ B _____
Camera _____ Enlarge _____ Reduce _____
Plate _____ No. of Burns _____ No. of Plates _____ % Screens _____

Product A
Stock _____ Wt. _____ Size _____ Colour _____
Trim Size _____ No. Up _____ Run Size _____
No. Out _____ Bleed _____ Sides Ink _____
Full Sheets Required _____
In Stock _____ On Order _____ Back Order _____

Product B
Stock _____ Wt. _____ Size _____ Colour _____
Trim Size _____ No. Up _____ Run Size _____
No. Out _____ Bleed _____ Sides Ink _____
Full Sheets Required _____
In Stock _____ On Order _____ Back Order _____

Pre-Press
Negs Shot _____ Negs Stripped _____ Plates Burnt _____
Stock Cut _____ Hold for Stock _____
Total Press Time _____ Initials of Printer _____
Number of Overs A _____ A Run _____
Number of Overs B _____ B Run _____

Bindery
☐ Fold ___ Places ☐ Perf ___ Places ☐ Score ___ Places
☐ Stitch ___ Places ☐ Trim ___ Sides ___ No. ___ to ___
☐ Drill ___ Places ☐ Collate ☐ Pad bks of
☐ Pad NCR ☐ Plastic Bind: Colour ___ Size ___
☐ Bundle of ___ ☐ Laminate

Package
☐ Wrap ☐ Box ☐ Carton ☐ Package for Transport

Special Instructions
(2)

OUTSIDE SERVICES
Company _____
Address _____
Telephone _____ Contact _____
Product _____ Date Out _____ Date Due _____
Quote _____ Shipped Via _____
(3)

Special Billing & Delivery Instructions
☐ Quotation Given ☐ Cash on Delivery ☐ On Account ☐ Client Called
Other _____

ACCOUNTS DEPT.
(1) _____
(2) _____
(3) _____
Subtotal _____
F.S.T. _____
P.S.T. _____
Less Deposit _____
Copy/Consult _____
Misc. _____

Grand Total _____

**EXHIBIT 5
QUALITY DESIGN AND PRINT LIMITED
FLOW OF INFORMATION**

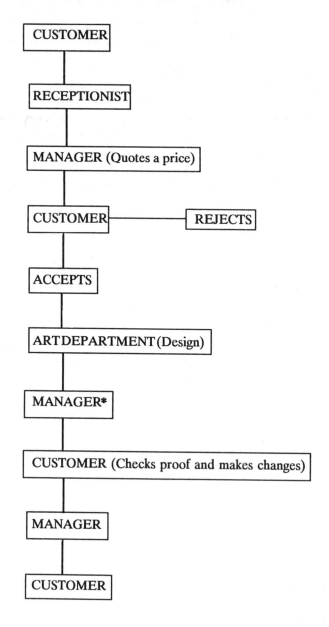

*A repeat order would start at this level.

EXHIBIT 6
QUALITY DESIGN AND PRINT LIMITED
WAGES (in dollars)

SALARIED POSITIONS	PER ANNUM
Owner*	25,350
Graphic Artist	18,000
Public Relations*	17,000
Press Dept. Supervisor	16,500
Art Dept. Supervisor	14,920
General Manager	14,625
Bookkeeper	13,650

HOURLY WAGES	PER HOUR
Typesetter	6.00
Receptionist	6.00
Press Operator	5.10
Press Operator	4.25

Based on a 37 1/2 hour work week with two weeks' vacation for each employee per year. Vacation pay is 4% of salary.

* Consulting related salaries

CASE 7

WESTERN INDUSTRIAL SUPPLIES

E. Gardner
The University
of Lethbridge
Lethbridge, Alberta

Lucy Carson took one last look at the files on her desk, which contained all of the information about the loans and the problems that she had as lending officer on the account of Western Industrial Supplies (Western). She reviewed mentally the events of the last eight years. Could something be done to save the company, she wondered?

BACKGROUND

Early in 1980, Western had made its first loan request to the Arctic Bank (the Bank) to help it establish itself. The owner wanted to purchase facilities and commit his time and effort to his business on a full-time basis. It was his intention to take second-hand plastic and brass parts and remanufacture them as custom-made parts and casings for industrial and agricultural use. The technological skills of the owner were clearly adequate to the task, although the equipment to be used was definitely not modern.

Financial plans, including sales forecasts, were not very definitive, but the owner expected to sell $300,000 to $500,000 per year in the first couple of years. Later years' sales were expected to exceed $1,000,000 and profits to increase more than proportionately. The use of the borrowed funds was, however, very clear: they were to be used to purchase a condominium warehouse to accommodate production and warehouse facilities.

The owner's equity was very small, being only about $26,750 in 1980. A loan of $90,000 was requested from the Bank in 1980 to purchase the warehouse, subject to the availability of additional financing from other sources. The owner was certain that such funds could be raised. See Exhibit I for the financial statements as at September 30, 1980.

The owner himself was a machinist who had, thus far, not had to manage more than a part-time business. His knowledge of his products was unquestioned, based upon his past experience as an employee in other companies, but his ability to operate his own business and to supervise people was unknown to the Bank.

BUSINESS DEVELOPMENT

Following the approval of the first loan application in 1980, a problem appeared. The additional financing to be obtained from other sources did not materialize. Given that the owner had already committed himself to the purchase of the condominium warehouse, he needed at least $30,000 more funding immediately. The Bank was asked to provide the funds, which were to be used for additional machinery and equipment to complete the facilities and place them in operation. Early in 1981 the loan was granted, with the machinery and equipment as collateral.

Financial statements for the years from 1981 to 1987 are found in Exhibit II. It is quite evident from this information that 1981 and 1982 were not successful years. The owner sought assistance before the financial condition of the business deteriorated significantly. The consultant who provided assistance indicated that the problems were not as much financial as personal. The owner had limited business skills and very poor interpersonal skills. Clearly, there was cause for concern. One area that was improved because of the consultant's advice was financial record-keeping. A more accurate financial picture was the result of the changes, as evidenced by the statements themselves.

In 1982, the owner decided that an expansion of his warehouse was necessary for inventory storage. He requested $75,000 in additional funds from the Bank for warehouse improvements, and the loan was granted. Despite the improvements, production was still inefficient and sales still lagged.

To obtain more space for production, the owner decided to purchase a second condominium warehouse. He obtained $210,000 from the Bank. The owner also granted to the Bank personal promises and personal property (real estate) of his own as collateral in addition to the second warehouse. The total indebtedness to the Bank now exceeded $390,000.

The basis for the loans on the second warehouse was the owner's forecast of $750,000 for sales in subsequent years. As Exhibit II shows, such sales never materialized.

The year 1983 was the best year for sales (other than 1986), but a loss still showed on the income statement. Full payment of interest and principal on loans was an almost impossible task. By early 1984, the loans were in arrears, creating a problem of serious concern to the Bank.

BUSINESS OPERATIONS

A number of different facets of the business operations bear examination in an evaluation of the strengths and weaknesses of the company.

(a) **Management**

The owner, Peter Schmidt, was a middle-aged machinist with extensive experience in Europe. He emigrated to Canada a number of years before he set up Western. His business skills were self-taught, and he was known to be a stubborn and strong-willed man. Apparently he had great difficulty in trusting other people and in listening to their advice. The other main employee was his wife, Wilhemina. Her part in the business was to answer telephones and handle the financial ledgers.

(b) **Other Personnel**

The business had few other employees. A number of casual workers were hired to assist in the production of goods when needed, but they never stayed on a permanent basis. The owner could not afford to keep them permanently because sales and production were so unstable. As a result, he was constantly training new people to operate the equipment.

(c) **Production**

Mr. Schmidt was in full control of production, machinery and equipment. The facilities had to be quite large to accommodate the equipment because of its size. The production machinery was not new, but it was efficiently run by Mr. Schmidt. He was able to keep it in good repair, and he always knew how to produce what his customers needed or wanted. His main problem was trying to explain to others what he wanted done.

The operations had to be supervised by Mr. Schmidt and, because of the lack of permanent employees, no one else ever learned how to run the machinery without him. This often meant that production had to wait while he was busy doing something else.

(d) **Sales and Marketing**

The company never had a full time sales representative other than Mr. Schmidt. Because he had full responsibility for production and sales, he had to split his time between the two functions. Sales were often the result of "word-of-mouth" because Mr. Schmidt never trusted dealers to sell for him. There were occasional sales trips to other parts of the country to find new customers, but these were only possible when other matters were not pressing. Most sales were made in small amounts to small- and medium-sized businesses directly through personal contact. No sales representatives or agents were ever employed.

Customers were pleased with the products and their quality, but they found that deliveries were often erratic. In addition, Mr. Schmidt required deposits and cash advances from customers to allow him to purchase raw materials for orders. There never seemed to be enough cash or lines of credit to keep the business running smoothly.

The forecasts of sales were heavily dependent on the sources for sales. Mr. Schmidt believed that the oil and gas and agriculture industries in the Prairies were his main customers, and consequently he had located in Alberta to be near them. The Bank depended on the sales forecasting of the owner when it made its loans, but he seemed to have no particular basis for his forecasts other than personal opinion. No statistical evidence was ever found to support them, nor was there any targeting of potential customers by promotional material or advertising. Selling seemed to be done on an "ad hoc" basis.

The collapse of both the oil and gas and the agriculture industries in the early 1980's had a major impact on Western. Mr. Schmidt tried to diversify into other product lines using the same equipment, but he had no real success because he was not familiar with the needs of potential customers.

(e) **Financial Plans and Controls**

It was quite evident that sales and profit forecasts were often wildly inaccurate. The owner and his wife had no real knowledge of finance and accounting. The outside accountant who prepared the annual financial statements was not asked to do anything else for the company, and he provided only what he was asked to do.

The Schmidt's obtained some outside assistance from a small business consultant, but it had a limited effect. Their intention was to improve the financial record-keeping in terms of timeliness and accuracy; there was a marked improvement in timeliness, but accuracy, especially in forecasting, remained a problem. The owner viewed financial statements at best as an inconvenience and at worst as an utter waste of his time. Outside of the bank statements and the detailed financial ledgers kept by his wife, no other records existed.

The Bank tried to make suggestions to Mr. Schmidt as to how to improve and expand the business, but he insisted on doing everything on his own without any outside interference. This was entirely acceptable as long as his payments arrived on time, but that was often not the case.

THE YEARS OF STRUGGLE

Beginning in 1984, Western fell behind on its loans to the Bank. When questioned, the response from the owner was always similar: he asked the Bank to have patience and all would be well. The only bright spot was an offer in 1986 to purchase the business. However Mr. Schmidt felt that the $150,000 price was unreasonably low, and he refused the offer. No other offer to purchase was ever received.

The difficulties in raising funds for working capital were compounded when suppliers threatened to cancel Mr. Schmidt's accounts because of erratic payments. All debt was now placed with the Bank, except accounts payable, and the Bank had first claim on all of the company's assets. The payment of accounts payable was only possible using customer advances because no other lines of credit could be obtained. With the Bank's permission, this was allowed so that the company could remain in business.

CASE REQUIREMENTS

The problems of this business create an interesting set of questions on which to focus:

(1) What mistakes, if any, were made by the Bank in providing financing?
(2) What, if anything, can be done to make the business viable, given the situation that now exists?
(3) What business practices should be changed and how can the changes best be made?
(4) Can sales forecasts and financial planning be improved and, if so, how?

These were the questions on the mind of Lucy Carson as she closed the files and started to prepare her report for her supervisor on what action to take next. Assume her role and deal with these issues.

EXHIBIT I
WESTERN INDUSTRIAL SUPPLIES
FINANCIAL STATEMENTS (in dollars)
September 30, 1980 (Loan Proposal Date)

ASSETS

Current Assets

Cash (in Bank)	2,000
Accounts Receivable	1,250
Inventory	4,000
Deposit On Property	7,500
Total Current Assets	14,750

Fixed Assets

Equipment	300,000	
Less Accumulated Depreciation	240,000	
Net Fixed Assets		60,000
Total Assets		74,750

LIABILITIES

Current Liabilities

Bank Loan	45,500	
Accounts Payable	2,500	
Total Current Liabilities		48,000
Shareholders Equity		26,750
Total Liabilities and Equities		74,750

INCOME STATEMENT

Revenues

Sales	70,000
Cost of Sales	43,700
Gross Margin	26,300

Expenses

Rent	4,500	
Automobile	1,200	
Utilities and Taxes	1,100	
Shop Supplies	1,600	
Repairs	1,800	
Telephone	250	
Travel	480	
Depreciation	9,000	
Total Expenses		19,930
Income from Operations		6,370
Less Interest		13,500
Net Loss		7,130
Gain on Equipment Sale		40,000
Net Income		32,870

EXHIBIT II
WESTERN INDUSTRIAL SUPPLIES
FINANCIAL STATEMENTS (in dollars)

BALANCE SHEET

ASSETS

Current Assets	1981	1982	1983	1984	1985	1986	1987
Cash	-0-	-0-	-0-	-0-	13,500	1,200	1,400
Accounts Receivable	14,400	30,300	56,500	25,500	21,500	48,500	63,500
Inventory	3,500	54,000	37,000	34,000	42,000	37,500	45,000
Due From Shareholders	-0-	-0-	-0-	12,000	-0-	-0-	-0-
Total Current Assets	17,900	84,300	93,500	71,500	77,000	87,200	109,900
Fixed Assets							
Automobile	1,500	1,500	1,500	1,500	1,500	1,500	1,500
Condominium Warehouses	135,000	375,000	375,000	375,000	380,000	380,000	380,000
Equipment	75,000	121,000	165,000	180,000	210,000	237,000	271,000
Less Accumulated Depreciation	-0-	-0-	26,500	51,500	78,000	106,500	136,000
Total Fixed Assets	211,500	497,500	515,000	505,000	513,500	512,000	516,500
Total Assets	229,400	581,800	608,500	576,500	590,500	599,200	626,400

LIABILITIES AND EQUITY

Current Liabilities	1981	1982	1983	1984	1985	1986	1987
Accounts Payable	7,000	67,000	87,000	69,000	95,000	62,000	93,000
Loan Payable	14,000	18,000	-0-	-0-	9,000	7,000	-0-
Bank Loan	37,000	37,000	70,000	60,000	37,000	7,000	-0-
Deposits From Customers	55,000	56,000	39,000	44,000	51,000	90,000	30,000
Interest Payable	-0-	-0-	-0-	-0-	-0-	-0-	14,000
Current Portion Of Long Term Debt	7,000	14,000	34,000	84,000	121,000	203,000	288,000
Total Current Liabilities	120,000	192,000	230,000	257,000	313,000	369,000	425,000
Long Term Debt							
Arctic Bank	108,000	395,000	431,000	455,000	492,000	446,000	495,000
Less Current Portion	7,000	14,000	34,000	84,000	121,000	203,000	288,000
Due To Shareholders	10,000	12,000	10,000	-0-	-0-	10,000	50,000
Total Long Term Debt	111,000	393,000	407,000	371,000	371,000	253,000	257,000
Shareholders' Equity	(1,600)	(3,200)	(28,500)	(51,500)	(93,500)	(22,800)	(55,600)
Total Liabilities and Equities	229,400	581,800	608,500	576,500	590,500	599,200	626,400

EXHIBIT II
WESTERN INDUSTRIAL SUPPLIES
FINANCIAL STATEMENTS (in dollars)

INCOME STATEMENT

	1981	1982	1983	1984	1985	1986	1987
Sales	90,000	145,000	245,000	192,000	205,000	405,000	170,000
Cost Of Sales	61,000	67,000	90,000	57,000	70,000	127,000	58,000
Gross Margin	29,000	78,000	155,000	135,000	135,000	278,000	112,000
Expenses							
Salaries	12,200	6,600	22,500	20,000	17,200	48,500	12,600
License and Business Property Taxes	3,000	3,000	6,600	12,300	13,200	18,000	1,600
Utilities and Condominium Fees	4,100	5,700	9,000	9,900	8,900	9,900	9,000
Shop Supplies	-0-	6,100	6,200	10,500	8,000	20,000	3,700
Automobile Supplies	3,800	3,400	3,700	3,700	2,500	2,200	4,400
Telephone	2,400	3,000	3,700	3,100	2,400	3,100	2,800
Travel	-0-	2,000	5,900	-0-	-0-	1,500	1,500
Consultants	-0-	1,800	1,200	-0-	-0-	-0-	-0-
Accounting Expenses	800	1,800	-0-	-0-	-0-	-0-	-0-
Office Expenses	-0-	-0-	1,200	1,100	400	2,100	1,500
Insurance	2,200	-0-	900	-0-	-0-	-0-	-0-
Legal Expenses	5,800	300	-0-	-0-	-0-	6,900	-0-
Repairs and Maintenance	6,000	-0-	-0-	-0-	-0-	-0-	-0-
Miscellaneous Expenses	1,550	600	2,900	3,400	3,900	8,100	1,200
Depreciation	-0-	-0-	17,500	17,000	17,500	19,000	20,000
Total Expenses	41,850	34,300	81,300	81,000	74,000	139,300	58,300
Income From Operations	(12,850)	43,700	73,700	54,000	61,000	138,700	53,700
Interest	15,500	36,300	84,000	62,000	83,000	49,000	77,500
Directors Fees	-0-	9,000	15,000	15,000	20,000	19,000	9,000
Net Income	(28,350)	(1,600)	(25,300)	(23,000)	(42,000)	70,700	(32,800)
Dividends Paid	-0-	-0-	-0-	-0-	-0-	-0-	-0-
Addition To Retained Earnings	(28,350)	(1,600)	(25,300)	(23,000)	(42,000)	70,700	(32,800)

MID-WESTERN PUBLISHING COMPANY PART (A)

V. Govindarajan
Dartmouth College
Hanover, New Hampshire

G.W. McClain, Jr. was sitting at the conference room table of the Mid-Western Publishing Co., talking rapidly. Only eight years earlier, just turned 25, and holding a newly-minted Harvard MBA, he had been brought to Mid-Western as Executive Vice-President. It had been McClain's first exposure to the printing industry. Not long thereafter, he had been named the company's President and Chief Executive Officer. Now McClain was excitedly discussing Mid-Western's replacement cost-based managerial evaluation system, saying, "I invented this system!"

HISTORICAL REVIEW OF MID-WESTERN PUBLISHING

In 1983, Mid-Western Publishing (MWP) was a 60-year old newspaper and printing holding company. Although Mid-Western was headquartered in a small town, operations also existed in several other small towns within its home state.

Mid-Western was a closely-held private concern. But the chairman of the board, a member of the owning family (no relation to McClain), was a U.S. Senator, and spent a great deal of time in Washington, D.C. In fact, McClain had found that he had a free hand in directing day-to-day operations.

Before McClain's arrival, Mid-Western had been loosely managed. The chairman, as a busy public figure, was rarely in the firm's offices, and the past president had not extracted adequate financial performances. The key area of concern for the company was asset utilization; asset returns were, in fact, not keeping pace with inflation. As a result, Mid-Western was not generating sufficient internal funds for asset replacement, and as McClain put it, "The company was cannibalizing itself," or, in a rural idiom, it was "eating its own seed corn."

Most of Mid-Western's assets had been acquired in the 1920's, with significant additions in the 1950's and 1960's. By 1983, its key assets included five sheet-fed printing machines and two web printing facilities (each costing hundreds of thousands of dollars). Intangible assets included name recognition among readerships, and a dominant position in a small town newspaper market. These assets were used in operations consisting of a dozen daily and weekly newspapers, and several commercial printing businesses. The newspapers served separate localized markets.

THE SITUATION WHEN McCLAIN ARRIVED

On January 3, 1976, when G.W. McClain joined Mid-Western Publishing, he began learning that a lot of hard work faced him. To that date, annual budgeting had never been performed at Mid-Western. Further, the management incentive system was not pressuring the operations managers for outstanding financial performances. McClain described the operations as he found them.

> In this company, every year, book value of investment was going down on a GAAP basis, and the volume of dollars (business) on book value was declining also. As a result, this company was undercapitalized.

Since McClain's total financial compensation was substantially dependent upon Mid-Western's financial performance, he set out to correct these problems.

McCLAIN'S REPLACEMENT-COST EVALUATION SYSTEM

As McClain considered how to improve the financial performance of Mid-Western, he examined the organizational structure, management incentives system, and financial objectives of the firm. As a result of the review process, McClain and Mid-Western's owners agreed that the firm should be earning 10% above inflation; in conjunction with setting of this new objective, McClain designed his new management controls package.

Prior to this time, Mid-Western had no targets for return on invested capital and, thus, there were no incentives to achieve any specific target. Managerial salaries were substantial with incentives for overall profit level achievement in nominal dollars which added a small amount to compensation. Assets were valued at historical cost book value and were not used for incentive calculations. There were no specific profit centres or responsibilities which could be used for the calculation of incentives outside of total profit figure.

Although the most innovative feature of the new system was the basis of evaluation of profit centre managers, McClain made other changes as well. The organizational structure was changed to include six "master" profit centres, with other profit, revenue, and cost centres within the "master" centres. Exhibit 1 provides an example of the new organizational structure in the "Citizen" division in Citizen, Indiana. Other changes of McClain's are summarized below:

(1) Sharply lowered profit centre managers' salaries.

(2) Increased the incentive compensation available to managers.

(3) Changed asset valuations, for managerial evaluation purposes, to replacement costs.

(4) Established "Corporate Obligations" for the six master profit centre managers.

(5) Set divisional performance objectives at inflation plus 10%.

Each of McClain's changes is reviewed in detail below:

Taken in tandem, the first two steps allowed McClain to establish aggressive incentive bonuses. The incentive bonuses were tied to the actual financial performances as measured by the corporate obligations. (See step 4.) The net result was to sharply increase the pressure on managers for improved financial performances, and this caused great turmoil among the profit centre managers at first.

As a third step, in order to provide higher goals for financial performance, McClain adjusted the asset valuations to incorporate inflation. Replacement cost valuations were based on replacement-cost data compiled by a department of the U.S. government. For example, a ten-year old web newsprint facility would be indexed to its current replacement-cost. McClain made an effort to adjust the data for the cost-increase effects of technological advancements. Financial assets were adjusted by the GNP deflator. All replacement-costs for a fiscal year were indexed by the prior year's inflation data.

From the above three steps, McClain then examined the earnings potential of each division ("master profit centres"), and established the Corporate Obligations for each individual division. These amounts were arbitrarily arrived at by McClain; the managers were only informed of their corporate obligation for the year. In relation to this, McClain commented, "They trust me, they really do." Below, the formulation of the Corporate Obligations is covered in more detail.

FORMULATION OF THE CORPORATE OBLIGATIONS

Corporate Obligations were described by McClain as consisting of two parts. Part "A" was an allocation of home office overhead, which included the following expenses.

(1) **Payroll**

(2) **Accounts Payable** – also centralized. Divisions were charged with the administrative expenses on accounts payable.

(3) **Auditors** – the expense of audits by outside auditing firms.

(4) **Insurance Benefits** – for employees of Mid-Western.

(5) **Disability Insurance** – especially necessary in the newspaper business, but more cost efficient in one central corporate policy.

(6) **Legal Expenses** of Mid-Western Publishing.

(7) **Interest Expenses** on long-term debt.

In explaining part A of the Corporate Obligation, McClain commented, "They (profit centre managers) have enough to do without screwing around with this stuff."

Part "B" of the Corporate Obligation was in essence a profit expectation placed upon the divisions, and was calculated by McClain from the Corporate Obligation worksheet. (See Exhibit 2.) Though the profit centre managers had a rough understanding of the factors used in the calculation of the Corporate Obligation, they were not aware of the specific criteria being applied to them. As McClain put it, "You have to sit here and play God."

In return for their efforts, profit centre managers received, in the form of a bonus, one-third of any cash operating income above the corporate obligation. There was *no* limit placed on the amount they could earn on this bonus. These bonuses were paid in the same form by which profit centre managers' results were evaluated: cash. In referring to this system, McClain said that profit centre managers were evaluated based on "money on assets," i.e., cash returns from asset utilization. On the other hand, he described himself as being rewarded on a "money on money" basis, i.e., total corporate cash returns on the cash invested in the company by its owners.

McCLAIN'S INCENTIVE COMPENSATION

As a part of the new management incentives package, McClain and Mid-Western Publishing's owners agreed on an incentive formula to reward McClain's efforts. Exhibit 3 details McClain's incentive compensation formula.

Exhibit 3 (Part I) is a conceptual representation of the formula. The "Home Office Bonus" was, in fact, McClain's bonus. As can be seen from the Exhibit, McClain's bonus was equal to one-third of the adjusted cash operating profits above that level of profits required to provide Mid-Western's owners a rate of return 10% greater than inflation. Note that this was based on the stockholders' equity account.

Exhibit 3 (Part II) presents, in more detail, the formula for McClain's incentive bonus. Again, it should be noted that his bonus was based on cash results, with the notable exception of the depreciation. McClain illustrated this ("money on money") by commenting that since the home office paid for all capital expenditures, which would then be reflected in the stockholders' equity account, his mission was to earn a maximum return corporate-wide.

THE "CITIZEN" DIVISION

The Citizen Division will be examined as an example of the new evaluation system at Mid-Western. As Exhibit 1 shows, the Citizen Division was one of the six master profit centres at Mid-Western Publishing.

Newspaper vs. Commercial Printing

Within the Citizen Division existed two distinct businesses: a dominant small town newspaper, and a commercial printing business. Both businesses utilized the same printing equipment. Since the success of each business was critical to the overall division performance, McClain made the two separate managers of each business a profit centre. Their bonus was a 50/50 split of any bonus available from the Citizen Division's cash operating performance compared with the Corporate Obligation requirement. According to McClain, this made each profit centre manager a "partner" in the Citizen Division, and forced them to cooperate in the utilization of the printing machinery and other assets.

The use of two separate profit centres within the Citizen Division master profit centre reflected the substantially different natures of the two businesses. The commercial printing business, on the one hand, was a highly competitive enterprise, with price as a key competitive variable throughout the commercial printing industry. Business for the commercial printing operations was not limited to the home state of Mid-Western Publishing, as a substantial portion came from out-of-state customers. Aside from the price, printing quality and meeting delivery schedules were also important factors for success in commercial printing.

The newspaper business, on the other hand, was different. Revenues came from both circulation and advertising. As the dominant newspaper, the Citizen had some flexibility in pricing, though advertisers could also use radio or other media. Critical to the success of the Citizen was local news coverage, along with feature stories of local interest. However, since the daily newspaper could be printed in one and one-half hours' press time, the commercial printing business was needed to help spread high fixed costs associated with the printing equipment. Within the Citizen profit centre, advertising was a revenue centre, circulation a sub-profit centre, printing a cost centre, and administrative expenses a cost centre.

Like all Mid-Western Publishing managers, the two managers of the Citizen Division had high autonomy. However, three types of decisions were routinely forwarded to CEO McClain for a "second opinion:"

(1) Firing of an employee.

(2) Hiring of key employees.

(3) Capital investments and major purchases.

A Recent Fiscal Year

To illustrate how McClain's system worked, some financial results of the Citizen Division are shown in Exhibits 4 to 7.

In summary of the Exhibits, each of the two profit centre managers of the Citizen Division earned a $29,536 bonus, in addition to their regular salaries, for their efforts. For his efforts, McClain earned a bonus of $76,949 in addition to his regular salary, from the Citizen Division alone. McClain himself had said,

> All I care about is cash. Divisions are given certain dollars in order to produce dollars. . . The divisions are like customers, and I am like the bank. . . Those certain dollars, and the amount they are required to return. . . that's the punch line to the job!!

This incentive system has caused some consternation among profit centre managers. Because their base salaries have been cut substantially, they are worried about the amounts of bonuses that can be earned under this new system. It needs to be evaluated to assess its impact on these managers in both the short term and the long term.

EXHIBIT 1
MID-WESTERN PUBLISHING COMPANY
MWP ORGANIZATIONAL STRUCTURE

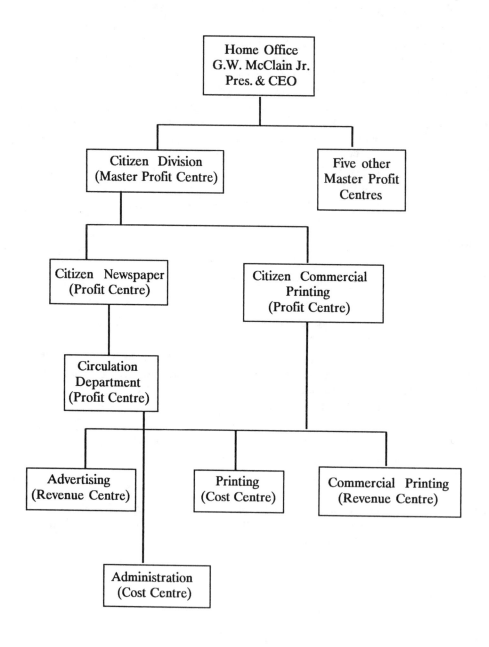

EXHIBIT 2
MID-WESTERN PUBLISHING COMPANY
CORPORATE OBLIGATION (in dollars)
("Money on Assets" for the Divisions)[1]

	Amounts
Expected Sales	
% Company Sales	
Corporation Expenses[2]	_____
	_____
Home Office Investment	
Net over 30 days' average accounts receivable of past 12 months	
Indexed value: machinery, fixtures & furniture purchased before 2/1/79	
Indexed value of furniture purchased after 2/1/79	
Indexed value of leasehold	
Original value (Gross Book Value) of machinery, furniture, leasehold, autos, land	
Total Home Office Investment	_____
Investment Factors	
12 months' average net over 30 days accounts receivable x GNP deflator	
9.09% x depreciation of machinery, furniture purchased before 2/1/79	
11.11% x depreciation of machinery purchased after 2/1/79	
12.5% x depreciation of furniture purchased after 2/1/79	
10% x dep. indexed leasehold inside 10 years	
10% on original value: cars, machinery, furniture, leasehold, land	
Total Investment Factors	_____
	_____
Corporate Expenses & Investment Factors Total	
Corporation Expenses	
Investment Factors	
Total Obligation	_____
Last Year's Given Obligation	_____
	_____

Notes

[1] *McClain's worksheet for Corporate Obligation calculation (what is referred to in the case as "money on assets").*

[2] *The expected corporate cash operating expenses are apportioned to the divisions based on the percentage of each division's expected sales for the coming year to the total expected company sales.*

© John Wiley & Sons Canada Ltd. All rights reserved.

EXHIBIT 3
MID-WESTERN PUBLISHING COMPANY
MCCLAIN'S "MONEY ON MONEY"
THE HOME OFFICE BONUS FORMULA

OVERVIEW

Home Office bonus equals one third of:
Annual adjusted cash operating profit
MINUS
Adjusted stockholders' equity as of
February 28/29 of the previous fiscal year
TIMES

> Ten percent return on investment
> ### PLUS
> The GNP deflator for the previous calendar year

DETAIL OF ABOVE

Total cash profits from divisions and all other cash investments and cash revenues

    Plus that year's revenues from other sources (i.e., non-operating revenues)

    Less that year's non-operating expenses

    Less total cash Home Office expenses before dividends, before prepaid and current federal income taxes and before Home Office bonuses.

    Less the previous year's straight line depreciation of buildings, capital assets, leasehold improvements and land improvements until fully depreciated (11 years on capital assets purchased prior to March 1, 1979; 9 years on machinery and 8 years on furniture purchased after March 1, 1979; 10 years on leasehold improvements, capital improvements and buildings as auditor determines) according to generally accepted accounting principles.

EQUALS
Annual adjusted cash operating profit.

EXHIBIT 4
MID-WESTERN PUBLISHING COMPANY
CITIZEN DIVISION CORPORATE OBLIGATION
(in dollars)

	Amounts
Sales	1,200,000
% of Corporate Sales	27%
Corporate Expenses Allocated	55,890
Home Office Investment	
Net over 30 days' Accounts Receivable, 12 Months' Average	11,300
Indexed Value: Machinery, Fixtures, and Furniture, pre-2/1/79	683,300
Indexed Value: Machinery, post-2/1/79	30,700
Indexed Value: Furniture, post-2/1/79	9,100
Indexed Value: Leasehold	179,300
Original Value: Machinery, Furniture, Leasehold, Autos, Land	416,700
Investment Factors	
12 Months' Net over 30 Days' A/R, avg., @ 5.8%	655
9.09% Depreciation of Machinery and Furniture, Pre-2/1/79	62.112
11.11% Depreciation of Machinery, Post-2/1/79	3,411
12.5% Depreciation of Furniture, Post-2/1/79	1,138
10% Depreciation of Leasehold	17,930
10% Return on Gross Book Value of Assets	41,670
Total Investment Factors	126,916
Corporate Expenses Allocation	55,890
Total Corporate Obligation	182,806

EXHIBIT 5
MID-WESTERN PUBLISHING COMPANY
CITIZEN DIVISION
STATEMENT OF CASH INCOME[1]
(in dollars)

Revenues	
Advertising, Net	493,200
Circulation, Net	107,800
Commercial Printing, Net	489,000
Total Revenues	1,090,000
Departmental Expenses[2]	
Editorial & News	211,200
Advertising	103,100
Circulation	91,900
Composing	137,500
Press & Platemaking	169,700
Administrative	126,400
Total Expenses	(839,800)
Net Cash Operating Profit	250,200
Other Income	
Gain on Sale of Fixed Assets	156,200
Less Other Expenses	
Cash Discounts Allowed	17,100
Interest Expenses	11,800
Loss on Sales of Fixed Assets	17,300
Net Cash Non-Operating Income	110,000
Net Cash Income	360,200

Notes

[1] *These statements were prepared monthly. GAAP basis statements were separate, and strictly for tax purposes.*

[2] *These were actual cash expenditures only.*

EXHIBIT 6
MID-WESTERN PUBLISHING COMPANY
CITIZEN DIVISION
MASTER PROFIT CENTRE BONUS (in dollars)

Net Cash Income	360,200
Less Corporate Obligation	182,806
Net Bonus Base	177,394
x factor (33%)	.333
Net Cash Bonus to Citizen Division	59,072
Per 2 Division Managers:	
Division Bonus x 50%	.5
Net Cash Bonus per Manager	29,536

EXHIBIT 7
MID-WESTERN PUBLISHING COMPANY
CEO'S BONUS PER CITIZEN DIVISION OPERATIONS
(in dollars)

Description	Amount
Total Cash Profits from the Citizen Division	250,200
Other Cash Income Less Expenses	110,000
Less Home Office Cash Expenses[1]	55,890
Less Previous Year's Straight Line Depreciation of Assets until Fully Depreciated[2]	39,340
Adjusted Annual Cash Operating Profit	264,970
Less: Stockholders' Equity x (inflation + 10%) = CEO's Obligation to Owners = $214,500 [3] x(.058 + .10) =	33,891
CEO's Bonus per Citizen Division	231,079
33.3% payout ratio	x .333
= CEO's Bonus per Citizen Division Operations	76,949

Notes

[1] *Before prepaid and current federal income taxes and before Home Office Bonus.*

[2] *11 years on assets purchased prior to 3/1/79; 9 years on machinery, and 8 years on furniture purchased after 3/1/79.*

[3] *The total stockholders' equity for the company was $1,287,000. Since there were six profit centres, 1/6th of the equity is shown here.*

Endnote

1. *Financial data are disguised and do not necessarily reflect actual division results.*

PART (B)

Bill Kirston sat behind his desk contentedly. As Managing Editor and Head of Mid-Western Publishing Co.'s largest operating division, he carried heavy responsibilities. His division was very profitable, with plans for significant expansion. Kirston was a veteran in his mid-fifties, who had substantial publishing experience and had been at Mid-Western for many years.

Things had not always gone so well for his division, however. Prior to G.W. McClain, Jr.'s arrival as President, his division had been "eating its own corn seed," earning insufficient real returns to finance operations over time. Inflation had destroyed the quality of the division's earnings, and it was unable to make necessary capital investments without external funding.

The solution to this problem proved to be McClain's replacement–cost evaluation system. Kirston had despised it at first; it was the cause of a cut in salary and increased pressures to perform. Looking back, however, Kirston readily conceded the system had brought his division back to life. "Profits" were now real profits, providing funds for new equipment and expansions.

Although Kirston's relations with McClain were currently good, they had not always been that way. McClain, the industry rookie who cut Kirston's salary under the new system, had caused radical upheavals in Kirston's life. But eventually Kirston came to view McClain as the "teacher" of these radical new management systems, and himself as the "student." He did not question the exact calculation of his "Corporate Obligation"; he knew only he must earn it in order to make a bonus and provide funds for his division's future. He knew also *that as a result* of McClain's system, his income had risen greatly.

The only remaining concern for Bill Kirston is whether he can continue to obtain these bonuses and maintain these income increases in the long term. He does not understand the system well enough to be able to assess its possibilities.

CASE 9

CURRY LIMITED

P. Clark
University College
Dublin, Ireland

Una Carroll sank wearily into her hot bath. Now that she was alone she finally had a chance to collect her thoughts and sort out her priorities.

Una had commenced practice on her own six months previously, two years after qualifying as a Chartered Accountant. During her training period, apart from her fair share of photocopying in the early weeks, she had obtained a good range of practical audit experience. However, Una felt that her real forte was in the field of accounts preparation and advising on the problems of small businesses. Although the firm she worked for had a small clients department, Una felt it did not offer the excitement and challenge she wanted. The decision to start up on her own was easy to make.

Two days previously Una had received a phone call from John Curry, who asked to see her urgently. John was an old friend from her days at college. In those days he had seemed to spend most of his time in the football club, but his hectic social life did not appear to interfere with his academic work. To the surprise of many, he graduated with a degree in polymer science. Since college days Una had lost contact with John although she knew that he had subsequently completed an MBA.

John had arrived promptly at 9:00 a.m. in Una's office. She was surprised — timekeeping had not been John's strongest point, but that was not the only thing that had changed in John. He was looking drawn and haggard and had lost his "laid back" air. After they exchanged reminiscences about their college days and nights, John came directly to the point of his visit.

"I'm under a lot of pressure at the moment," he said.

"Tell me about it," Una replied calmly.

© John Wiley & Sons Canada Ltd. All rights reserved.

"My father died last week. He had a plastics business on the outskirts of town. He was working late one night and must have had a stroke."

Una remembered reading the death notice in the local paper, but had not associated it with John.

"Things are a bit hectic at the moment as a result."

Una anticipated what was coming.

"I need your professional assistance," John said. "The account books aren't up to date. The staff are uneasy, but I think that I can sort it out, given time. Customers keep ringing up asking about deliveries and the bank manager is anxious that everything should be fixed up as soon as possible."

Una interrupted him, "Who's your accountant?"

After a slight pause John replied, "Dad spent all his time on administration and did all the books himself, but he hadn't written them up for some time. Of late, he seemed to spend most of his time chasing customers for money. I have the last two years' accounts which should give you an idea of our financial position." John passed a slim file across the table (Appendix 1).

Una took the file and briefly glanced through it. She noted the current auditor. "Des Daily, Accountant and Auditor," the bold type had proclaimed to the world. Des had a flourishing practice specializing in small family businesses. He was efficient in the sense that the books were returned quickly, and he was cheap, a fact appreciated by his clients.

"I'm not very happy with his work and would much prefer to have someone like yourself going over the books. Dad used to say that Des based his fee on a percentage of sales. Perhaps we could come to a similar arrangement," John added sincerely.

Una looked John straight in the eye.

"Have I said something wrong?" he asked.

Una replied by asking John about the business and its background. The firm had been started by John's father about fifteen years ago. It manufactured polyethylene one-piece moulded products such as garbage containers and fuel containers, which were sold to wholesalers throughout the country. John believed that the firm could beat any competition in terms of quality and price.

John continued, "Last February Dad persuaded me to join the business. We decided to widen the range of products with the addition of plastic drainpipes and eavestroughs supplied to builders, and the do-it-yourself market via supermarkets and hardware dealers, where it was anticipated that margins would be higher than those achieved previously."

He continued, "Due to technical problems with the new products, we had some production difficulties and higher than normal wastage was incurred. Initially I spent most of my time on the production end trying to sort out the problems. Towards the end of the year I concentrated on the marketing side of the business. We invested $96,000 on a special promotion and advertising campaign for the new range of products. The benefits are beginning to emerge and we will reap the real benefits over the next few years. For example, we operated at normal capacity this year and 90% of our output was sold by the end of the year. We also sold all our opening inventory apart from a special lot which I'll explain later. We're making progress and all I need is time."

Una was prepared to accept that John's optimism was backed by determination. She then asked John what provision his father had made regarding the transfer of the business.

"Dad left the business to me and the house and contents to my elder sister. He had nothing else, not even a company pension. Mother died when I was eighteen, just before I went to college. I had always intended to come back and gradually take over the business and let the old man retire. Then this happens. I've no ties now with the business or this town, apart from yourself."

Una felt herself blush, but was pleased at this latter piece of information.

John added, "It wouldn't take very much of an offer to get me to sell lock, stock and barrel but I don't know what the business is worth. What I need is objective, professional advice. Could you come over to the factory and see for yourself?"

The following day Una arrived at the offices of Curry Ltd. at the prearranged time. The plant consisted of a single-storey building which was about fifteen years old. The land had been purchased by the late Edward Curry when he first started his business. At that time it had been well out of town, but during the intervening period a well-developed residential area had grown up around the plant, to such an extent that the factory could not be expanded beyond its present size. Some of the plant and equipment looked very new. Una was shown into Edward Curry's office where John was waiting for her.

"Dad was going over the books when it happened, probably getting ready for the annual audit. Our year end is 31 December. Have a look for yourself."

Una started to look around. On the desk she found some notes and files.

"That's a start, a list of Accounts Receivable and Accounts Payable at the year end. I wonder, did your father take stock as well?"

"Terry Walker might help you there," said John.

Terry Walker was the storeman. After the introductions Una asked whether an inventory count had been done on 31 December. "Sort of," was the reply.

It transpired that Des Daily had never attended the annual inventory count and simply relied on the figures supplied to him by Edward Curry. Raw material prices were taken from recent suppliers' invoices and the raw material valuation amounted to $42,000 at the end of the year. The valuation figures for finished goods inventory were always done by Edward Curry.

That afternoon Una and John called at the bank to pick up bank statements of the business up to 31 December, 1987. These were the most up-to-date ones available, and she also received all paid cheques which would allow her to analyze recent cheque payments. She was shown into the manager's office.

"Dreadful business!", the bank manager exclaimed. "I knew old Edward well, we helped him out at the beginning of the year. An astute businessman in his day, but, of late, things did not seem to be going so well. I intended to invite him in for a chat. He didn't seem to be able to get money in. Mind you few of the local businesses can. We hold the deeds of the land and buildings as security. The local auctioneer has certified for our files that the place is worth about $300,000 at today's prices."

Una looked at the bank statement balance at 31 December 1987. It was $6,000 overdrawn.

On the way home Una asked John whether his father had been worried about anything before he died.

John responded, "There were a few things, really. For one thing he was personally short of cash. He took a small salary each month from the firm and then on occasions would take cash out of the till. He was also upset about a special deal that went sour last year. About fifteen months ago we manufactured, on a one-time-only basis, some plastic moulds for a local firm. At the last moment the company went into liquidation, so we were left with surplus stock on our balance sheet last year at a cost of $15,000. He spared no effort in trying to get rid of it. Recently he got two offers to sell but they don't seem attractive. The offers are still open. I'll give you the file when we get back to the office (Appendix 2). Recently a claim was made against us for the sale of defective products. Personally, I think the claim is incorrect, but the amount of money involved is considerable."

Later that evening Una returned to her office and pondered the task ahead. The first step was to prepare a set of draft accounts for the year ended 31 December, 1987; then she could tackle the other problems. She spent the rest of the evening analyzing and summarizing the cash and bank transactions. She was grateful that at least the bank account reconciled exactly. With the help of the previous year's accounts and the additional information which she had gathered (Appendix 3), she set about the preparation of the current year's file.

CASE REQUIREMENTS

From the information given

1. Prepare a draft profit and loss account for the year ended 31 December, 1987 together with a balance sheet at that date.

2. Write a memo to John Curry analyzing the performance of the company, highlighting the key problem areas. You should also advise him in relation to the various issues which he discussed with you.

3. Prepare a memorandum for your file listing any other issues which should be discussed with and/or mentioned to John Curry.

APPENDIX 1
CURRY LIMITED
SUMMARIZED INCOME STATEMENTS
For the Years Ended 31 December (in dollars)

	1985	1986
Sales	460,000	504,000
Less Cost of Goods Sold:		
Material Costs	254,000	278,000
Direct Labour	82,000	96,000
Production Overhead including Plant Depreciation	26,000	28,000
Gross Margin	98,000	102,000
Less Other Expenses:		
Administration & Entertainment	36,000	42,000
Distribution	9,000	10,000
Interest	8,600	10,200
Depreciation – Vehicles	600	600
Depreciation – Fixtures	600	500
Advertising	18,000	20,000
Net Profit for Year	25,200	18,700
Add Prior Year's Balance	4,000	29,200
	29,200	47,900

BALANCE SHEETS
As At December 31 (in dollars)

	1985	1986
Assets		
Current Assets		
Stock – Raw Materials	16,000	28,000
Stock – Finished Goods	52,000	66,000
Accounts Receivable	56,000	88,000
Bank – Current Account	8,200	4,000
Cash	1,800	3,000
Fixed Assets (Net)	82,000	72,400
Total Assets	216,000	261,400
Liabilities and Equities		
Current Liabilities		
Accounts Payable	94,800	121,500
Term Loans	72,000	72,000
	166,800	193,500
Common Shares ($2 each)	20,000	20,000
Retained Earnings	29,200	47,900
Shareholders' Funds	49,200	67,900
Total Liabilities and Equities	216,000	261,400

APPENDIX 2
CURRY LIMITED
OFFERS RE DISPOSAL OF SURPLUS INVENTORY
(in dollars)

1. Costs already incurred in the production of the special order.

Direct Materials/Labour	13,600
Manufacturing Overhead: Variable	1,200
Manufacturing Overhead: Fixed	200
Allocation of Other Fixed Costs	1,800
	16,800
Agreed Price	30,000
Deposit Paid (and forfeited in October 1986)	3,000

2. Offer From **KAYTELL COMPANY** (received October, 1987)

Sales Bid Received	24,000
Additional Identifiable Work (Estimated)	
Direct Materials/Labour	5,000
Production Overhead — Variable	440
Production Overhead — Fixed	1,060
Allocation of Other Costs — Variable	1,000
Allocation of Other Costs — Fixed	3,400
	10,900
Costs Already Incurred	16,800
Total Costs to Date	27,700
Anticipated Loss	3,700

   Status: Existing customer, with good credit rating.

3. Offer From **DUNNE & COMPANY** (received November, 1987)

Sales Bid Received	22,000
Additional Identifiable Work (Estimated)	
Direct Materials/Labour	4,200
Production Overhead — Variable	400
Production Overhead — Fixed	1,060
Allocation of Other Costs — Variable	1,800
Allocation of Other Costs — Fixed	1,400
	8,860
Costs Already Incurred	16,800
Total Costs to Date	25,660
Anticipated Loss	3,660

   Status: New customer with the possibility of additional sales.

APPENDIX 3
CURRY LIMITED
NOTES MADE BY UNA

1. Cash taken for Edward's personal expenditure was taken from cash received from debtors and no record of this expenditure was kept. However receipts were always issued to trading debtors. An analysis of the cash receipts together with bank receipts and payments based on bank statements to 31 December, 1987, reveals the following (in dollars):

Receipts issued to customers	762,000	(prior to banking)
and deposits therefrom	754,400	per bank statements
Bank term loan received	20,000	per bank statement
Cheques paid to suppliers	414,600	per bank statement
Total expenses (analysis below)	347,800	per bank statement
Purchase of motor vehicle	22,000	per bank statement
Cash on hand 31 December 1987	400	

Details of Opening and Closing Balances	1 Jan. 1987	31 Dec. 1987
Trade accounts receivable (gross)	88,000	110,000
Trade accounts payable	121,500	76,800

The closing bank balance per the bank statement amounted to $6,000 overdrawn. Unpresented cheques paid to suppliers amounted to $5,000, while there was an outstanding deposit of $3,600.

Analysis of Total Expenses

Production Labour	124,000
Production Overhead	22,800
Administration Expenses	58,800
Special Advertising	96,000
Normal Advertising and Promotion	16,800
Charitable Contributions	1,000
Entertainment Expenses	7,000
Distribution Costs	9,200
Bank Interest	12,200
	347,800

2. Extra from Fixed Asset Register at 1 January, 1987 (in dollars)

	Plant & Equipment	Fixtures & Fittings	Motor Vehicle	Land & Buildings	Total
Cost 1 Jan. 1987	80,000	18,000	6,000	40,000	144,000
Less Accumulated Depreciation	56,000	13,800	1,800	nil	71,600
Book Value	24,000	4,200	4,200	40,000	72,400

Annual Depreciation Rates are as follows:

Plant, equipment and motor vehicles — 10% on cost with a full year's depreciation being provided in the year of purchase but none in the year of disposal.

Fixtures and fittings — 10% on a reducing balance method.

3. During the year a loss on equipment was incurred caused by scrapping all calibrating equipment not in metric sizes and which had no further use or benefit. The book value at time of disposal was $16,000 (i.e. $28,000 − $12,000).

4. Subsequent to the year end, one of the company's major customers (Alpha Ltd.) went into liquidation. At 31 December, 1987 the balance due was $18,000. The liquidator was appointed on 14 January, 1988 and the balance due was then $26,000. The liquidator had confirmed that there were insufficient funds to pay any of the ordinary creditors.

5. During the year it was discovered that finished goods included in inventory at the 1986 year end were incorrectly valued. The error in overvaluation has been identified at $22,000.

6. A claim has been made against the company for the sale of defective products. The company, which is not covered by insurance, is contesting the claim and expects to be successful in its defence. The amount of the claim is $120,000. However, in the unlikely event that the defence might be unsuccessful, it is estimated that the amount payable would be between $70,000 and $90,000. (More precise information is unavailable.)

CASE 10

TVFI CASE

J. Brackner
Utah State University
Logan, Utah

(Monday, 10 a.m.)

JB: (CEO) Hi, Charlie, come on in and close the door.

Charlie: (CFO) Thanks, JB. Betty (secretary) just caught me and said you wanted to see me.

JB: Yeah, I have a proposal for you to evaluate for us. I played golf Saturday with Bob Atwood (a local attorney friend) and he introduced me to a friendly old gentleman named Ray Dewey. Ray is a farmer and it seems that a couple of years ago he was within one day of starting to harvest his plums when a rainstorm came. The drying of the rain caused the plum skins to split, making them unfit to pack and ship to the East Coast markets. So Ray decided to harvest them anyway, pit them with his cherry-pitting equipment, and freeze them for alternate marketing. The only trouble was that there was no alternate market that he could find and he had 300 tons of the stuff costing him $1,500 per month storage.

Charlie: That would be an interesting dilemma. What did he do?

JB: Well, he talked with some guy in the Food and Nutrition Department at Brigham Young University (BYU) who experimented with the plums and developed a dehydrated fruit product that is really tasty. This guy at BYU expanded the experimentation project and came up with some other flavours. He developed apple-cinnamon, apricot, cherry, and grape products to go with the plum, and Ray has just started to market these products as fruit bars.

Charlie: This sounds like a real success story. Where do we fit in?

JB: Well, you know Bob. He had an ulterior motive for getting me out to play golf. He knew we were successful in making and distributing candy bars, and he and Ray want us to distribute the fruit bars. As you know, our strategic plan is to be vertically integrated and I didn't feel good about taking on a project of distribution without having more control over its source, so I countered by asking how much he would sell the venture for. From the 15th to the 18th green Ray kept saying, "Let me think about it." As we went to the clubhouse, Ray said that he would get me more detailed information and a price. Bob just brought this packet of information from Ray and I would like you to evaluate it and let me know what you think we should offer for it, or if we should even consider buying it.

Charlie: The auditors are in doing some preliminary work right now. It will probably be tomorrow or Wednesday before I can get to it. Let me review this material and I'll meet with you Thursday morning.

(Thursday morning)

Charlie: Good morning, JB. Do you have some time to review that fruit-bar venture?

JB: I sure do. Come on in.

Charlie: I reviewed that packet of materials from Ray Dewey and the following are the excerpts of the information he sent:

1. The asking price is $700,000.

2. What we will receive is the stock of a corporation (TVFI) with a tax loss carry-forward of $120,000, 300 tons of plums in cold storage with a basis of $60,000, some experimental equipment with a basis of $35,000 used to make the test bars, plus the results of various research efforts including the secret formula for making the bars. As an alternative, we can purchase the assets instead of the stock at the following market values: plums at $120,000, experimental equipment at $40,000, and the secret formula at $540,000.

3. At the present time, 1 oz. fruit bars are being produced on a small experimental system and are sold at 19 cents per bar. It is anticipated that the normal wholesale price will be 18 cents per 3/4 oz. bar, and the demand for the first year will be between 7 million and 12 million bars. If $100,000 per year is spent on advertising, sales are expected to increase by 12% per year for the first five years.

4. **Product:** Dehydrated fruit bars (candy or health food).
   Flavours: Apple, apricot, cherry, grape, and plum.
   Formula: One hundred pounds of wet, raw product will yield 33 pounds of dry, finished product. There is also an 11% loss in preparing the raw fruit for dehydration.

   Contents of wet product are:

Fruit Solids	87 lbs.
Sugar or Syrup Solids	12 lbs.
Ascorbic Acid	1 lb.
Flavour Enhancer	2 oz.
Total	100 lbs.

The fruit solid is a secret mixture of different fruits with apple being the primary ingredient in most of the products. The fruit cost in the following estimates reflect the weighted-average costs of the secret mixture. The probability relates to the cost shown above the probability.

	Packaging Quality (just before ripe)			Ripe (available one month each year)		
	High	Mean	Low	High	Mean	Low
Fruit:						
Cost	$600/ton	$560/ton	$500/ton	$400/ton	$380/ton	$350/ton
Probability	15%	75%	10%	20%	65%	15%
Sugar or Corn Syrup Solids:						
Cost	$500/ton	$445/ton	$400/ton			
Probability	10%	70%	20%			
Ascorbic Acid:						
Cost	$.03/lb	$.025/lb	$.02/lb.			
Probability	20%	55%	25%			
Flavour Enhancer:						
Cost	$4.00/lb.	$3.80/lb.	$3.20/lb.			
Probability	30%	40%	30%			

5. A reputable engineering firm has indicated that a two-year-old drying machine (reported to be in excellent condition), which cost $550,000 new, is available in a bankruptcy sale for $75,000. This machine can process 450 lbs. of finished product per hour. An additional $100,000 is needed to transport and set up this equipment for production, and it will take three months to get it set up properly. It should last for 15 years. Additional cost for support equipment is $275,000. This equipment can be purchased or leased for seven years at $55,000. If leased, there is an option to buy at the end of seven years for $20,000. This machinery has an expected life of 15 years.

   The maximum number of bars that can be produced during the first month is 300,000.

6. A building is available for rent at $1,650 per month or 1% of sales, whichever is greater. We also have an option for three years to purchase the same building (which has an expected life of 20 years) for $150,000. Other expected costs are:

Direct Labour	$.016 per 3/4 oz. bar
Packaging	$.020 per 3/4 oz. bar
Fuel, electricity, water, etc.	$.007 per 3/4 oz. bar
Shipping	$9.00 per 100 lbs. of finished product
Employee fringe benefits	30% of direct labour and salaries
Administrative salaries	$100,000 per year
Annual (November) property taxes	$10,000
Insurance	$38,000 per year

   It is anticipated that costs will increase on an average of 5% each year.

7. The present cold storage cost of $1,500 per month or $5 per ton per month will continue until the plums are removed.
8. This company will pay taxes on profits, at a 35% rate. All sales are on terms of 2/10, n/30. All purchases are on terms of n/10 days. The building available for buying or leasing has adequate cold-storage facilities to hold enough fruit to process for one week. We can obtain daily shipments of fruit from our vendor, who is 20 minutes from our facilities. A hurdle rate of 12% after taxes is used to measure potential investments.

Charlie: As you know, we are in a tight cash situation and, if we pay $700,000 for this venture, we won't have any money on hand for working capital. I can arrange with our bank a $650,000 line of credit at prime plus 2% adjusted quarterly. I plan to build a microcomputer spreadsheet template that will forecast the cash flow and net income on a monthly basis, but I wanted to review what I have with you first to make sure my assumptions are realistic.

CASE REQUIREMENT

Identify all ambiguities, list the issues to be resolved, and suggest their best solutions before developing the cash-flow and income forecasts. After completing the forecasts, use them to test the possibilities of success of this venture and write a report with a recommendation of whether to purchase it or not.

CASE 11

THE CASE OF THE MISSING PROFITS

D. Knutson
University of Wisconsin
Eau Claire, Wisconsin

David Kindschi, CPA, has been retained by Moore Manufacturing Co. of Centerville, Wisconsin to act as an expert accounting witness in a civil lawsuit. Moore Manufacturing is being sued by Ahmad Industries for damages related to an alleged breach of contract. Ahmad Industries is a soft drink bottler located in the tiny island country of Brailand. Kindschi has been informed that Morey Lester, also a CPA, has been retained by Ahmad as their expert accounting witness.

Lester has prepared a pretrial report which indicates that Ahmad Industries had, as a result of Moore's alleged breach, lost profits totalling $6.5 million. Kindschi has been instructed to review Lester's report with a "critical eye" and to prepare a pre-trial report of his own concerning what amount, if any, of lost profits resulted from the alleged breach of contract.

BACKGROUND

Brailand

Brailand is a small independent island country located in the Middle East. Because of its oil revenues, there has never been any sort of income or sales tax in Brailand. The exchange rate between its currency and the U.S. dollar has remained virtually constant for the last 15 years. Accordingly, all monetary values in this case have been expressed in U.S. dollars.

Ahmad Industries

Ahmad Industries is the major bottler of carbonated soft drinks in Brailand. The company has been in the soft drink business since 1950.

Allen Ahmad, son of the founder Amon Ahmad, has been its chief operating officer since 1972.

Moore Manufacturing Company

Moore Manufacturing is the second largest manufacturer of bottling lines in the United States and has competed in world markets for over 30 years.

THE CONTRACT

Early in 1977, Ahmad Industries entered into a contract with Moore Manufacturing to buy a new 65-spout bottling line for $1.2 million. The stated reason given for this acquisition was that the "aging" 60-spout line then in operation at Ahmad was inadequate to meet the rising consumer demand in Brailand for carbonated soft drinks. The new line was to be on-line at the beginning of March 1979 in plenty of time for the peak 1979 summer season.

For various and disputed reasons the 65-spout line was not ready for operation by the target date. In fact, after several years of dispute, Ahmad rejected the bottling line in December 1982. No saleable production was ever achieved on the line. Ahmad continued to use the old 60-spout line throughout this period, and a new German bottling line was purchased and installed in 1984.

THE LAWSUIT

Ahmad Industries has filed suit for damages related to Moore's alleged breach of contract. Many legal issues are to be resolved (including whether or not a breach has occurred). However, the issue addressed by Lester (and to be addressed by Kindschi) relates only to the question of "lost profits."

LESTER'S REPORT

Following are the pertinent portions of Lester's pretrial report.

> At the request of counsel for Ahmad Industries, I have reviewed the calculation of their claim against Moore Manufacturing Co. for damages related to lost profits. The following paragraphs and schedules describe this claim and my review of the calculations presented in its support. The total claim for lost profits is $6,473,500.
>
> **Sales Estimates**
>
> I was informed that Ahmad's reason for contracting to purchase the 65-spout line was to replace the existing line and at the same time provide for additional bottling capacity necessary to meet increased consumer demand for carbonated soft drinks. The old line had reached its capacity and was no longer able to produce in quantities sufficient to maintain Ahmad's share of the growing Brailand market.
>
> **Machine Capacities**
>
> According to the specifications outlined in the contract prepared by Moore Manufacturing, the new line was rated at 1,850 cases per hour. The old line had a rated capacity of 1,475 cases per hour. I was informed that total production

hours for a year are approximately 2,881. This estimate allows for maintenance and holidays.

On this basis, the calculated annual capacity of the old line was 4,249,475 cases. However, production time and calculated capacity are lost through flavour changes, power failures, bottle washing, bottle breakages and start-up and stopping. Line efficiency is therefore less than rated capacity. In 1978 actual production was 3,413,173 cases and, accordingly, actual line efficiency was approximately 80.32% of rated capacity.

The 65-spout line had a rated capacity of 5,329,850 cases. However, practical capacity based on line efficiency of 80.32% (assuming similar production characteristics as the old line had in 1978) would be 4,280,936 cases. Based on prior experience and market estimates, management concluded that with the 65-spout line, sales would have increased as the market increased and that the ability of the new line to provide the product to meet those sales would have been reached by the end of 1983 through its reaching practical capacity in its operations during that year. The old 60-spout line had been purchased in 1973 and had reached its capacity in 5 years.

Potential 65-Spout Line Sales

Based on that premise, the additional capacity of 867,763 cases per year that was to have been supplied by the 65-spout line would have resulted in an average annualized sales increase of 173,553 cases for the period March 1, 1979 through December 31, 1983.

Total estimated potential sales from the 65-spout line during this period were estimated at $49,245,400 (See Schedule A.) based on such annualized sales increase evenly attained year by year during that period expressed at actual sales values per case. This assumes an average increase of about 4 1/2% in sales each year.

Review of Sales Projection

To determine the reasonableness of Ahmad's estimated potential sales calculations I reviewed the past history of their sales statistics and the Brailand growth statistics discussed below.

Past History

Ahmad Industries Case Sales (000)

1970	1,337	1977	3,230
1971	1,453	1978	3,413
1972	1,544	1979	3,005
1973	1,630	1980	2,945
1974	1,574	1981	3,232
1975	1,932	1982	3,049
1976	2,484	1983	2,437

Going back to 1970, Ahmad shows a growth rate of approximately 12% per year over the eight years prior to the loss period. For the five years prior to the loss, they had increases of 16% per year. Clearly, the assumption of a 4 1/2% increase during the loss period is reasonable given the company's prior experience.

SCHEDULE A
THE CASE OF THE MISSING PROFITS
ESTIMATED POTENTIAL 65-SPOUT LINE SALES
March 1, 1979 through December 31, 1983 (in dollars)

	Cases	Sales Value
Practical Capacity		
65-Spout Line	4,280,936	
60-Spout Line	3,413,173	
Total Additional Capacity	867,763	
Annual Increase in Sales Over 5 Year Period	173,553	
Estimated Potential		
65-Spout line sales		
(old 60-Spout line as base year)		
1979 (3/1-12/31) *	3,210,120	7,349,500
1980	3,760,279	9,400,700
1981	3,933,832	9,834,600
1982	4,107,385	10,268,500
1983	4,280,938	12,392,200
Total	19,292,554	49,245,500

* *Full year 1979 = 3,586,726 cases (3,413,173 plus 173,533). Period March 1 to December 31 = 3,210,120, factor of .895 for 10 months.*

Brailand Population and Money Supply Growth

I also reviewed statistics published by the government of Brailand. The statistics indicate that for the ten years 1971 through 1981, the population grew at an average of 5% per year. Also, from 1976 to 1981, the Brailand money supply increased an average of 16%+ per year. The 4 1/2% projected sales increase is very reasonable when compared to these statistics.

Lost Sales

As a result of the failure of the new line to supply the growing market, it is estimated that Ahmad suffered a sales loss totalling $12,869,800 for the period March 1, 1979 through December 31, 1983 (estimated potential sales of $49,245,500 less actual sales of $36,375,700).

Percentage of Profit and Contribution to Fixed Overhead

To estimate the amount of profit and contribution to fixed overhead that would have been generated by the lost sales, I reviewed actual financial results of Ahmad for the years 1979 through 1981. These results were obtained from financial statements which were audited by Brailand public accountants.

Based on my experience as a CPA, I identified those expenses that vary with sales and estimated the amount of variable costs and expenses that would have been incurred had Ahmad actually produced the extra sales of $12,869,800. These costs and expenses include materials and supplies consumed, production labour and benefits, and variable overhead expenses (including selling and administrative expenses). Actual variable costs during the three years, as thus identified, were 49.7% of actual sales for that period. By deduction, the remaining 50.3% of sales value represents profit and contribution to fixed overhead on incremental sales.

The application to estimated lost sales of $12,869,800 of this 50.3% contribution results in an estimated profit loss of $6,473,500. Schedule B (below) summarizes this calculation.

SCHEDULE B
THE CASE OF THE MISSING PROFITS
CALCULATION OF LOST PROFITS AND
CONTRIBUTION TO FIXED OVERHEAD (in dollars)

Sales — March 1979 through December 1983	
Estimated Potential	49,245,500
Actual	36,375,700
Sales Lost	12,869,800
Calculated Profit and Contribution to Fixed Overhead Percentage	50.3%
Calculated Loss of Profit and Contribution to Fixed Overhead	6,473,500

KINDSCHI'S ANALYSIS

Kindschi, after a careful review of Lester's report, had a number of nagging doubts about it. He gathered some additional information to help him in preparation of his own report. A summary of this additional information follows.

Seasonality

Kindschi learned that the soft drink market was very seasonal in Brailand (similar to the United States). Chart I presents Ahmad's sales (in cases) on a monthly basis for the period January 1, 1978 through December 31, 1983.

Competition

Inquiry as to the market in Brailand revealed that there were only two other competitors in the carbonated soft drink market. Both competitors (CW Distributors and SU Products) were considerably smaller than Ahmad. No imports of carbonated soft drinks were allowed in Brailand. No exports of this product had occurred through the end of 1984.

Kindschi was able to secure sales data (in cases) from an officer of CW Distributors. These data are also presented in Chart I. No data were available from SU Products.

Although no details were available, Kindschi also learned that a new non-carbonated fruit drink had been introduced in Brailand in the mid 1970's. This product was sold in 6 oz. bottles at a lower price than that of carbonated soft drinks.

CHART I
THE CASE OF THE MISSING PROFITS
COMPARISON OF MONTHLY SALES OF
AHMAD INDUSTRIES (AI) AND CW DISTRIBUTORS (CW)
(000 cases)

	1978		1979		1980		1981		1982		1983	
	CW	AI	CW	AI	CW	AI	CW	AI	CW	AI	CW	AI
Jan.	32	169	47	142	38	103	47	124	53	130	51	128
Feb.	32	151	50	176	40	110	49	150	47	115	52	123
Mar.	45	222	61	242	60	200	63	222	58	165	62	167
Apr.	60	297	81	304	79	257	80	288	82	271	78	257
May	91	342	90	330	83	294	85	340	103	363	102	366
June	108	365	80	326	81	378	87	318	80	339	63	259
July	111	424	69	292	64	332	67	285	70	308	58	237
Aug.	70	320	57	266	73	336	87	391	89	384	65	252
Sep.	82	338	80	296	80	261	93	358	93	351	59	224
Oct.	92	334	81	297	84	300	95	304	96	331	na	192
Nov.	64	254	61	195	71	239	77	254	65	158	na	139
Dec.	53	197	47	139	54	135	69	198	49	134	na	93
	840	3413	804	3005	807	2945	899	3232	885	3049	na	2437

Price

Kindschi learned that in Brailand the price of all products is set by the government. The wholesale price for cases of carbonated soft drink had been set at $1.974 from 1972 until June 1, 1979; at $2.50 from June 1, 1979 until June 1, 1983; and $3.289 after June 1, 1983. Retail prices are also controlled and were increased at the same time as wholesale prices.

Product

All carbonated soft drinks in Brailand are sold in 10 oz. bottles. Over 80 percent of Ahmad's sales were of a cola flavoured soda — the rest of the sales consisted of a lemon-lime soda, an orange soda, and a white soda. The relative popularity of these flavours varied very little over the years.

Equipment Failure

Kindschi also investigated statistics concerning the number of hours that the old 60-spout line had been inoperable because of equipment failures. He found that the line had been inoperable during normal production times a total of 176 hours for the period from March 1, 1979 through December 31, 1983. He found that in only five months there were more than five hours of down time due to equipment failure (September 1979 – 12 hours; February 1981 – 23 hours; October 1981 – 10 hours; February 1983 – 8 1/2 hours; and May 1983 – 66 hours).

Profitability

Kindschi obtained the following financial data related to Ahmad for the period 1970 through 1982 in thousands of dollars ($000).

Year	Sales	Operating Profit	Year	Sales	Operating Profit
1970	2,638.8	370.5	1977	6,375.0	1,609.5
1971	2,867.8	374.2	1978	6,866.8	1,297.4
1972	3,047.4	278.4	1979	6,893.9	1,671.8
1973	3,217.1	195.8	1980	7,362.4	2,112.4
1974	3,106.6	599.7	1981	8,080.0	1,722.4
1975	3,813.2	700.5	1982	7,622.4	1,558.7
1976	4,902.6	1045.9	1983	7,054.5	na

Rationing

Kindschi reviewed the transcript of Allen Ahmad's deposition. Ahmad testified that he had been forced to ration his product among his customers throughout the period 1979 through 1983. He stated that he found it necessary to turn down customer requests for additional product "hundreds of times each year."

Inventory Policy

Ahmad's inventory records indicate that inventory was usually kept at a level high enough to cover four to six days of sales. Furthermore, Kindschi determined that Ahmad had only run completely out of inventory on two occasions between 1979 and 1983 (in February 1979 and in May 1983) and then for only one day each time. Kindschi also determined that carbonated soft drinks have a shelf life of at least six months, that refrigeration is not necessary, and that cases of soft drinks can be stacked 12 cases high.

Labour Availability

Finally, Kindschi learned that Ahmad operated two shifts during the peak season and one shift during the remainder of the year. Six-day work weeks are the norm in Brailand. Much of the labour force in Brailand consists of foreign nationals from India and a few other countries. Apparently, there was no shortage of such labour.

CASE REQUIREMENT

Draft a report on behalf of Kindschi to Moore Manufacturing with regard to the issue of "Lost Profits." As part of your analysis, identify Lester's key assumptions and respond to them. Be explicit about your own assumptions.

CASE 12

STRATHCONA PUBLIC SCHOOL BOARD

C.R. Batch
Wilfrid Laurier
University
Waterloo, Ontario

J. Fisher
Wilfrid Laurier
University
Waterloo, Ontario

J. McCutcheon
Wilfrid Laurier
University
Waterloo, Ontario

At two o'clock on Tuesday afternoon May 17, 1988, Mary Smith, a school trustee, was preparing for that evening's meeting of the Area Board of Education, which is the independent body responsible for operating the public schools. The main topic for the meeting was the fate of Strathcona Public School. For the last six months various Board Committees had examined in depth a staff proposal to close the school, among other possibilities, in order to maximize use of Board resources; the final vote was due this evening. Ms. Smith was distressed by the high level of emotion and the confrontation between the Board staff and the community that had accompanied the whole process. It seemed that every statement and disclosure made by Board staff was being questioned by members of the community. Moreover, community leaders were questioning the motives of the Board and its staff in initiating the closure proposal. Ms. Smith wanted to make her decision this election year in a manner that was best for the taxpayers and also best for the seemingly forgotten factors in the whole process — the pupils at Strathcona and other schools in the area.

The Board staff had initiated the closure proposal last spring in hopes of avoiding heavy capital expenditures for fire code upgrading and building renewal purposes. The Board was aware that if Strathcona were

© John Wiley & Sons Canada Ltd. All rights reserved.

closed then the remaining core schools would operate at a much higher percent of student capacity, with some operating cost savings. In accordance with Board policy, a School Closure Committee was struck to examine the proposal and make recommendations to the Board; the committee was composed of six trustees and two senior staff members. When the proposal to close the school became public knowledge, the Community reaction was predictably one of outrage and a "Save Strathcona School" group was quickly organized.

Strathcona Public School is located in the core of a medium-sized city and has been an important part of city life for many years. The school was constructed just prior to the First World War and is considered by many to be of major architectural and historical significance. The building is large (22 rooms) and is certainly far beyond the size required now for a neighbourhood school. The school site itself is an extremely valuable piece of property which overlooks a large park. During the recent real estate boom unsolicited offers were received for the bare site that were in the range of $1.5 million. Although the boom has since abated, the school site is still of major value.

Strathcona is one of five public schools located in the core area. Enrolments as a percentage of capacity in these schools are quite low in comparison to the Board average of approximately 95 percent. (See Exhibit 1.) In fact, at some schools in new suburbs enrolments are over 100 percent due to the use of portable classrooms. The figures for Strathcona (about 38 percent capacity) are somewhat misleading though, as the School is used to capacity for educational purposes such as Adult Education. (However, the guideline issued by the Province only recognizes elementary school usage when determining capacity utilization.) First-time visitors to Strathcona are often taken aback by all the activity present, when they had expected only echoing halls. Of the five core schools, Board staff expect that only Queen Alexandra will show a major enrolment increase over the next five years.

The schools' catchment areas are neighbourhoods that were for the most part built before the First World War; many of the houses are more than one hundred years old. The neighbourhoods have traditionally been blue collar, with a pocket of expensive housing on the fringes of the park near Strathcona School. In recent years there has been a steady inflow of academics and professionals who are upgrading and renovating old homes. Consequently, the pupils come from a wide spectrum of economic backgrounds. A further feature is the rapid turnover of students who come to the area and then move away in short order. This is especially the case with new immigrants, who typically make up 10 percent of the Strathcona School population.

Four of the five schools, in common with many older schools, do not meet the new fire code requirements. If the schools remain in use as elementary schools there is no immediate legal requirement to meet the code, but if the buildings change use, then compliance is required immediately. Furthermore, many of the school gymnasiums, while considered adequate years ago, are below the size which is now considered reasonable. The school yards are also below standard, although this is mitigated by the fact that most schools are adjacent to parks.

The School Closure Committee met several times, both in public and in closed session, and held two open house sessions. As part of the process, the Committee commissioned an architect's report to study the capital costs involved. The directions to the architect were to examine the costs of upgrading the Strathcona facilities to meet the fire code and to estimate the costs of changing the facilities to house the elementary school on the bottom two floors and adult education facilities on the upper two floors. The elementary school renovations would include construction of a new gymnasium. The report is summarized in Table A.

TABLE A
STRATHCONA PUBLIC SCHOOL
SUMMARY OF CAPITAL COSTS FOR STRATHCONA SCHOOL
(in dollars)

1.	Upgrade to meet fire code	370,000
2.	General internal and external renewal	700,000
3.	Gymnasium and other elementary school costs	420,000
	Total	**1,490,000**

At the same time, Board staff prepared for the Closure Committee an estimate of the operating savings that would result if the school were closed (Table B).

TABLE B
STRATHCONA PUBLIC SCHOOL
SAVINGS IF STRATHCONA ELEMENTARY SCHOOL CLOSED
(in dollars)

Salary and Benefits*

Principal	60,000
Librarian (half-time)	25,000
Remedial Teacher (half-time)	20,000
Custodian	34,000
Total Salaries and Benefits	139,000

Building Costs

Utilities (40% of total utilities can be saved)	9,000
Maintenance **	18,000
Custodial Supplies	3,000
Total Building Costs	30,000
Total	**169,000**

* These are not transferrable positions; all other staff are transferred to other schools.
** Allocation based on average of all elementary schools.

Based upon the financial and other considerations the School Closure Committee voted to recommend to the full Board that Strathcona School be closed. Community reaction to the decision was extremely hostile, and organized. Moreover, the City Council, which is a different government body, strongly stated its own opposition to the closure; one City alderman criticized the School Board for being apparently more interested in land speculation than in education. The City undertook to aid the neighbourhood, first, re-zoning the school site as low density residential and second, offering to pay up to $500,000 towards the cost of a new gymnasium if the school was kept in use. The Board's capital figures were challenged as being excessive and it was suggested that all that was necessary, at least in the short run, was to deal with the fire code items. A further criticism of the closure proposal was that Adult Education was expected to grow and require more rather than less classroom space. Finally, the community challenged the enrolment figures that the Board used, claiming that they overlooked a new city-sponsored housing project. The Board staff did concede that the project might add about 40 students to Strathcona.

One of the most emotional aspects of the closure debate was that of the safety of the students. Without Strathcona, about 140 students would have to walk along routes that were either across four major arterial roads and the city core or across major streets and a busy railway line. The obvious solution to the problem was bussing, which costs about $750 per year per student ($24,000 per bus/32 student capacity). The Board itself only pays for 28 percent of the cost of bussing with the remainder a provincial government responsibility. The entire cost of crossing guards is a city responsibility with the incremental total being about $18,000 if Strathcona were to close. Cost savings would be similar for other schools.

A final complication in the debate about closure of Strathcona is that several parents have threatened legal action if the Board votes to close the School. The Board's solicitor seems optimistic, but she did point out that the legal ground on which the challenge appears to be based could also have an impact on the religious observances issue which had just been settled after months of controversy. Staff are saying that this is an important matter of principle which must be defended, and the settlement is a hard-won victory that should not be easily given up.

CASE REQUIREMENT

Ms. Smith wants to make her decision based upon full and accurate information, and she feels that she does not have it as yet. She therefore wishes to make a complete analysis of the closure decision and other alternatives before the meeting this evening. Assume her role and make the analysis and the decision.

EXHIBIT 1
STRATHCONA PUBLIC SCHOOL BOARD
CURRENT AND PROJECTED ENROLMENTS

	Effective Capacity	1987	1988	1989	1990	1991
Sir Arthur Currie	530	432	435	440	445	450
Prince Charles	476	354	360	365	370	375
Queen Alexandra	446	240	267	281	283	298
Strathcona	547	207	207	215	225	225
Wellington	570	337	330	325	324	323
	2,569	1,570	1,599	1,626	1,647	1,671

EXHIBIT 2
STRATHCONA PUBLIC SCHOOL BOARD
STUDENT ASSIGNMENTS IF STRATHCONA IS CLOSED

	Effective Capacity	1987
Sir Arthur Currie	530	432 + 60 = 492
Prince Charles	476	354 + 5 = 359
Queen Alexandra	446	240 + 62 = 302
Wellington	570	337 + 80 = 417
	2,022	1,570

Enrolment as a % of Capacity: 77.6%

EXHIBIT 3
STRATHCONA PUBLIC SCHOOL BOARD
1987 COSTING (in dollars)

	Strathcona	Currie	Prince Charles	Queen Alexandra	Wellington
Enrolment	207	430	354	243	339
Rated Capacity	547	530	476	446	570
Instructional Costs					
Instructional Salaries	443,548	762,751	638,455	632,471	740,202
School Administration Salaries	72,319	78,288	76,250	72,640	76,876
Travel Expense	251	122	850	143	224
Supplies	13,642	27,130	23,971	18,813	21,867
Telephone	2,037	1,785	1,675	1,746	1,074
Repairs	103	329	143	137	352
Total Instructional Costs	531,900	870,405	741,344	725,950	840,595
Cost Per Pupil (Instructional)	2,570	2,024	2,094	2,987	2,480
Building Costs					
Utilities	22,816	26,707	20,668	23,001	23,271
Custodial Salaries	45,960	58,647	56,188	57,303	62,307
Custodial Supplies	2,798	4,398	3,230	2,643	4,736
Snow Removal	813	929	1,705	2,081	1,201
Building Insurance	1,167	1,543	1,226	1,422	1,853
Total Building Costs	73,554	92,224	83,017	86,450	93,368
Cost Per Pupil (Building)	355	214	235	356	275
Maintenance Costs					
Building & Grounds	18,154	92,470	13,732	19,105	5,842
Total Maintenance Costs	18,154	92,470	13,732	19,105	5,842
Cost Per Pupil (Maintenance)	88	215	39	79	17
Total Cost	623,608	1,055,099	838,093	831,505	939,805
Total Cost Per Pupil	3,013	2,454	2,367	3,422	2,772

© John Wiley & Sons Canada Ltd. All rights reserved.

EXHIBIT 4
STRATHCONA PUBLIC SCHOOL BOARD
CAPITAL EXPENDITURES SCHOOL BY SCHOOL
ACTUAL AND PROJECTED
1987 – 1991

School: Sir Arthur Currie — Built 1936, additions 1950, 1956

Last Year (1987) (actual)
Paving $8,000; Main Panel $10,000; Off-Oil Conversion $12,000

This Year (1988) (estimate)
Heating Controls $7,000; Masonry $30,000; Ceiling $6,000

1989 (estimate)
Traps $3,000; Fire and Building Code $650,000

1990 (estimate)
Nil

1991 (estimate)
Heating Controls $5,000

NOTE *This school requires a new gymnasium.*

School: Prince Charles — Built 1955, additions 1957, 1966

Last Year (1987) (actual)
Roofing $27,000; Main Service $8,000

This Year (1988) (estimate)
Fire Alarm $2,000; Flooring $6,000

1989 (estimate)
Traps $3,000; Flooring $6,000

1990 (estimate)
Flooring $6,000

1991 (estimate)
Flooring $7,000; Windows $80,000

EXHIBIT 4 (continued)
STRATHCONA PUBLIC SCHOOL BOARD
CAPITAL EXPENDITURES SCHOOL BY SCHOOL
ACTUAL AND PROJECTED
1987 – 1991

School: Queen Alexandra – Built 1905, addition 1960

Last Year (1987) (actual)
Masonry $10,000; Off-Oil Conversion $12,000

This Year (1988) (estimate)
Windows $69,000; Main Panel $7,000

1989 (estimate)
Hot Water Regulator $6,000

1990 (estimate)
Pneumatics $2,000

1991 (estimate)
Heating Controls $3,000

NOTE *This school requires major fire code expenditures.*

School: Strathcona – Built 1911, additions 1920, 1929

Last Year (1987) (actual)
Off-Oil Conversion $11,000

This Year (1988) (estimate)
Fire and Building Code $1,356,000; Lighting $2,000

1989 (estimate)
Heating Controls $6,000; Traps $4,000, Ceiling $5,000

1990 (estimate)
Windows $30,000; Painting $20,000

1991 (estimate)
Masonry $42,000; Roofing $29,000

EXHIBIT 4 (continued)
STRATHCONA PUBLIC SCHOOL BOARD
CAPITAL EXPENDITURES SCHOOL BY SCHOOL
ACTUAL AND PROJECTED
1987 – 1991

School: Wellington – Built 1857, additions 1874, 1922, 1980

Last Year (1987) (actual)
Fire and Building Code $307,000; Off-Oil Conversion $10,000

This Year (1988) (estimate)
Heating Controls $13,000; Windows $35,000

1989 (estimate)
Painting $20,000; Flooring $7,000; Traps $3,000

1990 (estimate)
Flooring $7,000; New Panel $2,000

1991 (estimate)
Flooring $3,000; Pneumatics $2,000

CASE 13

CARBUCAL

A. Carrera
Instituto de
Altos Estudios
Empresariales
Buenos Aires,
Argentina

It was late on Thursday, March 3, 1986, and a meeting that was supposed to take only one hour was stretching into two.

JULIAN MONTALVES: (New head of Mendoza Plant 1)

"I think my position is the right one, and we should consider that the variable cost of each ton of coal consumed today by my plant is $4.44, not considering the freight. Anyway, if I do not consume the coal, it has to be sold at that price to someone else."

HORACIO FERRERO: (General Accountant)

"Julian, you don't have to worry about the cost assigned to it. You're only responsible for the amount of coal consumed per ton of carbide obtained. The rest is a matter of accountancy and nothing will change if we go on assigning money to it as we have until today."

JULIAN:

"I don't agree that this is just a matter of accountancy. I only know that the other plant (San Juan) is making profits and instead of $9.67, only $7.06 are assigned to it — it doesn't seem right."

GERMAN BARREIRO: (Head of San Juan Plant 2 and former head of Mendoza Plant)

"I don't think that, as long as the plants consume in a balanced way, we should make differences regarding assignments, and besides, wasting time over endless discussions about the costs takes us nowhere. Or is the total cost going to change because we are discussing things? But let me remind you, I'm not prepared to acknowledge more than $7.06 per consumed ton."

"Going into another subject, I hear rumours that we may get an additional order of carbide, provided that my plant is more modern and has a lower grinding cost at an equal coal cost. I haven't got the slightest doubt that if we do get the order we should make the carbide ourselves."

JULIAN:

"Sure, if I give you financial help it is convenient, but the other plant should be closed if it is less efficient and more costly."

At this point the three turned to the General Manager, Fernando Sima, for his opinion. Not sure about the issue of cost assigning or about the future of the two plants, he said:

> "Well, we're running overtime here and I think it's time to stop now. Let's all think about it over the weekend, and meet again Monday at 2:00."

THE COMPANY

Carbucal, founded in 1930, is a company devoted to the production of calcium carbide. The main offices are in San Juan, Argentina, and its two plants are in San Juan and Mendoza. Carbucal is an electro-intensive company, for whose operations the variable costs are coal, lime, transportation and electric power; the rest can all be considered fixed costs.

The company buys coal that is processed in the drying and grading plant situated in a petrochemical park near Mendoza city, and then takes the coal to plant 1 (situated in Mendoza state, 200 km away) and to plant 2 (which is in San Juan state, 100 km away). Plant 2 was located in San Juan because of a special price for electric power.

In the plants, lime (bought from a third company) is mixed with coal in the following proportions: 1 ton coal and 0.9 lime per 1 ton useful carbide. Then this is processed in the electric furnaces. Generally Carbucal sells carbide at the factory packed in disposable tin barrels; therefore, distribution of the product is easy.

MARKET CONDITIONS

The Argentinian calcium carbide market has been going through a critical period, as plant capacities exceeded total demands and a strong price war was going on. At the same time the PVC market (main user of calcium carbide, which is the raw material for PVC) was facing foreign competitors, which made the calcium carbide consumers keenly aware of prices.

Carbucal had been selling only 1,000 tons a month, of which 900 tons went to one customer and were produced in equal amounts by both plants; the company is at the economic break-even point.

As a consequence of market conditions, Carbucal customers kept asking for a quotation before they enlarged an existing order or before making a new one, generally asking competitors for a quotation as well. Another factor Carbucal had to consider was that its main customer was heading towards an integration process wherein calcium carbide would not be necessary. This would be carried out from new plants and equipment.

There is a possibility of keeping the present plant at work, depending on the income, which is being strongly affected by the cost of carbide. Carbucal's main competitor, with which it shared the market approximately 50–50, had anticipated this integration movement and diversified its product quite successfully. The diversification was based on the improvement of furnaces previously used and designed for the production of carbide.

FERNANDO SIMA'S DOUBTS

The General Manager had learned that his main customer had the possibility of winning a contract for some PVC, and Fernando expected to be asked to quote for some additional tons of carbide. Other companies had tentatively suggested the possibility of bidding for the contract, and one competitor in particular was a serious threat. It was estimated that the order would be about 500 tons.

Concerned about the issue of costing and wanting to be prepared to meet these possible orders, he called his accountant back to help him answer the following questions:

(1) Today our company supplies, nearly exclusively, one customer that buys at the factory. Would there be any possibility of lowering the production costs if the production were programmed in a different way? I wonder if it is acceptable for us to absorb the fixed costs of both plants, considering the present-day levels of production. I am convinced that at some level it would be more profitable to operate with only one of them, but which is that level and which plant should it be?

(2) At what price should we quote 500 additional tons of calcium carbide sold at the factory if we want to obtain a 10% margin over sales, considering that the direct administrative costs will be 4% of sales?

Fernando also wondered how the recent power price increase had affected San Juan. When the project was created they had a preferential price for electric power of $0.008 kw/h. But in the meantime this preference had been lost, and $0.016 kw/h were being paid.

Before setting to work the accountant gathered additional and more detailed information about the company's operation. First of all, he drew a simple diagram of the production process. (See Figure 1.)

PRODUCTION PROCESS

The Coal Plant

The coal classification plant was used to grade and dry the coal that would be the raw material for the production of calcium carbide. The process consisted of:

(1) Receiving the coal as it is from delivery trucks at a price of $5.33 per ton.
(2) Carrying it over to the drying plant at a price of $0.22 per processed ton.
(3) Drying the coal to get rid of the undesired moisture. For this step, 10 litres of gas-oil per ton were required. Gas-oil was generally bought at $0.02 per litre.
(4) After the drying step the coal was taken to the grading department at a cost of $0.11 per ton.

(5) The grading plant operated with a power cost of $3.33 per hour, and it was considered normal that it should process 10 tons every hour.

(6) After the grading plant step, the following production was obtained:
   20% of a grain between 0 and 2 mm
   40% of a grain between 2 and 4 mm
   40% of a grain bigger than 4 mm.

(7) From this plant the coal was carried in bulk to San Juan and Mendoza. The price per kilometre was $0.01 per ton.

As the technology used in the San Juan plant was different from the one used in the Mendoza plant, the types of coal they could take in were different. While the plant in San Juan could only use coal bigger than 4 mm, the Mendoza plant could use any coal bigger than 2 mm.

The first two types of coal already mentioned (0-2 mm and 2-4 mm) could be sold as industrial wastes and sub-products at the rate of $2.78 and $4.44 per ton respectively.

The plant normally worked in a single shift. The fixed costs of personnel and other expenses were $2,222.22 a month, whereas the amortization expenses amounted to $1,111.11 a month.

The personnel worked 25 days a month at a rate of six hours per shift. It was estimated that running another shift would mean increasing the personnel and other expenses by 80% over the existing levels.

The Mendoza Plant

With a production capacity of 1,000 tons a month of calcium carbide, materials were supplied in trucks from the coal plant and from the lime supplier, and taken to the factory. The price of lime is $3.33 per ton.

The calcium carbide production process starts at the furnace. For this step, 1 ton of coal and 0.9 tons of lime are required per ton of carbide. This process consumes 3,000 kw/h per ton; the price of each kw/h was $0.009.

The grinding is done on the cakes obtained from the already cooled melts, which adds some $1.11 per ton.

The grading is carried out from the ground carbide according to the sales specifications. It was usually possible to sell all types of grain at quite a uniform price. The grading machine had a monthly amortization of $111.11 and the personnel that worked it were paid independently from the level of activity in the amount of $444.44 a month.

Finally the packing is carried out, in 100 kg barrels bought in the market at $0.17 each. The personnel in this department also work in 6-hour shifts. There is a direct relationship between the number of workers and the packed production. For 500 tons per month of operation, six workers are required, which means a $333.33 expenditure a month, including employee benefits. For larger productions, more personnel can be hired hourly, at a rate of approximately one person-month for every 100 tons.

Apart from the expenses already mentioned the plant had to face $2,222.22 a month spent on fixed items, among which was the amortization of the furnace.

It is estimated that, if necessary, the plant operation could be stopped but $1,111.11 a month in fixed expenses would still remain, including amortization of the grading plant at $111.11.

The San Juan Plant

With a capacity of 50% more than the Mendoza plant, and being located closer to the coal plant, the only cost differences for the San Juan plant were the fixed costs that amounted to $3,333.33/month, and the grinding cost which, being that of a more modern plant, was lower and equal to $0.56 per ton.

This plant could also stop working if necessary, but there would still be $1,333.33 expenses a month on maintenance, security and amortization ($888.89).

After looking in detail at the production process and costs, the accountant asked himself some questions:

(1) What is the variable cost of a ton of useful (dry and graded) coal?

(2) What cost should be considered if the only coal used is coal bigger than 4 mm?

(3) If 500 tons of additional coal were required, 50% of it 2-4 mm big and 50% bigger than 4 mm, what would be the monthly cost of that lot?

(4) What are the variable costs of each plant per produced carbide ton, not taking into consideration the coal, but taking into account the freight?

(5) What would be the production cost per additional ton for each plant?

LATE EVENTS

On Monday morning the General Manager, who was in possession of the figures the accountant had given him, got two pieces of news. The first confirmed his predictions: Carbucal had just received a request to quote "your best price" for 500 additional tons of carbide. The second confirmed his fears: his main customer was seriously considering the possibility of integrating. He would have to adjust the price so that the plan for integration lost its attractiveness. It was vital that he and his people clearly understand all the figures because hard times were coming and they would have to make some important decisions about the future of Carbucal.

CASE REQUIREMENT

Analyze the cost and profitability of the two plants. Consider the potential closing of either or both and the long term effects. Also examine the overall market potential now and in the future.

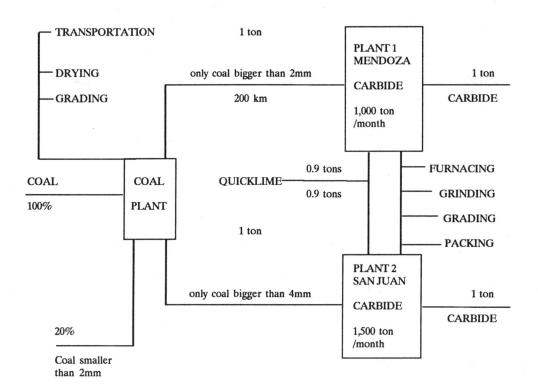

FIGURE 1
CARBUCAL
PRODUCTION PROCESS

CASE 14

JEAN'S PLACE

E. Gardner
The University
of Lethbridge
Lethbridge, Alberta

Jean and Sam Jones sat at a table in their restaurant (Jean's Place) on Saturday morning just before opening for business in Farmtown, Ontario. A number of thoughts crossed their minds as they surveyed the restaurant that they had operated for the last 30 years. One of their greatest concerns was their ability to keep operating the business because of their declining health. Sam, 58 years old, and Jean, 57, were both finding themselves less able to work the long hours needed in the restaurant, and they were depending more and more on the rest of the staff to run it. In particular, Sam had recently had a heart attack which had forced him to rest for several months, and Jean had wanted to spend the time with Sam rather than in the restaurant.

BACKGROUND

Jean's Place was a steak and seafood restaurant with seating capacity of 300 in the restaurant and an additional 120 in the licensed lounge. It catered to a regular middle class clientele in Farmtown, a city of 300,000 in Central Ontario. The restaurant regularly received a high rating in the AAA and Mobil Travel Guides, thus also ensuring a significant tourist trade.

Originally Sam Jones had been in partnership with four others in the operation of the restaurant, and Jean Brown (now Sam's wife) had been hired as the hostess. Gradually the other partners sold out to Sam until 15 years ago he became the sole owner. When Jean had been hired, the name of the restaurant had been The Farmtown Steakhouse. But when Sam and Jean married two years later and she began to take greater control of the operation, the name and menu started to change. The present format evolved over the years from discussions between Sam and Jean.

Except for a few months off during the first three years of their marriage to have two children, Jean has been hostess and, for the last 25 years, restaurant manager. Sam had been the manager at first, as well as part-time chef, but, as the business developed and Jean took a more active role with the customers, Sam became more involved in the kitchen as chef and more actively pursued other business interests in his spare time. He seemed to be quite content to let his wife run the restaurant since it was very successful without his direct involvement anywhere except the kitchen.

Sam now owned the restaurant land and buildings, the adjacent office building, other properties in Farmtown and a 300 acre farm in the country with a large house on the farm property. Although Sam visited the restaurant or worked in its kitchen almost every day, he also spent considerable time on his farm. Hired employees actually operated the farm for Sam, but he and his wife lived in the house on the property.

BUSINESS OPERATIONS

Facilities

The restaurant is located on a main thoroughfare of Farmtown with extensive parking facilities adjacent to the building. On the opposite side of the parking area is an office building rented to doctors, dentists and lawyers with a pharmacy in the lower level. The parking lot is shared since Sam Jones owns both buildings. Across the street is a small apartment building which is owned as a rental property. There are several other rental properties, also owned by Sam, scattered throughout the city.

The farm is a separate operation from the restaurant, office building and rental properties, and Sam and Jean plan to keep it for retirement. Sam and Jean are seriously considering the purchase of a winter home in Florida, but they have taken no action to find one. Jean has become more persistent in her requests that Sam do something about it. It is very likely that Sam and Jean will buy one in the coming winter because Sam has run out of excuses to put it off.

Clientele

Jean's Place has never been a trendy or upscale restaurant, but rather it serves an established clientele ranging from young families to senior citizens. Prices and menu selection are always reasonable for all ages and most income levels.

Similar or "copycat" restaurants have come and gone in Farmtown, but Jean's Place continues to thrive. There are no special gimmicks that have been tried, but the decor and furnishings are upgraded every few years so that the appearance does not detract from the restaurant environment. The main reason that customers return appears to be the first class service that is the trademark of the establishment. Jean and Sam Jones insist upon prompt and courteous service from the staff, and they make no apology for firing employees who do not maintain the restaurant's reputation for excellence. From her first day as hostess Jean was a stickler about customer service, and she has not lowered her standards over the years. It was this characteristic that drew Sam's attention to her from the beginning, and he continues to admire her for it.

Menu Selection and Service

Jean's Place offers a variety of steak and seafood items prepared under the supervision of either Sam or Charlie Lee, the other experienced chef, who has been with the restaurant for more than 20 years. The menu is occasionally varied to add new items or to remove slow-moving ones, but the main items have been on the menu for at least 10 years. There is also a children's menu for families that come to the restaurant.

The restaurant features a self-serve salad bar which is available as an option for any entree on the menu. Appetizers and entrees are brought to the table by the staff. Also featured is a selection of desserts which are brought to the table on a cart by the staff. Holidays are often featured at the restaurant and special family occasions such as birthdays, anniversaries and graduations are willingly handled as long as the group can be accommodated without undue inconvenience to regular customers. The lounge is separated from the restaurant area so that noise levels are reduced in the restaurant itself, and the restaurant area is actually separated into three parts, each of which is accessible to the others, to the bar and to the kitchen. The pace of the operations is such that the customers are unhurried, but the staff are constantly active. The host or hostess always tries to check with customers, especially regular ones who are known by name, to see that everything is pleasant and enjoyable. Mistakes or complaints are promptly rectified.

Personnel

The two owners (and the main employees for many years), Sam and Jean Jones, have nurtured the operation from its infancy, starting from 75 seats (bar and restaurant combined) and growing to the present 420. They have raised it just like it was one of their children, and, indeed, they consider many of the employees to be like family.

Although Sam and Jean's two children worked in the restaurant while they were in high school and university, neither is involved now. One is a lawyer and the other is an accountant. Both live in other cities and seem content to stay there. Neither has any ownership share in the restaurant.

Charlie Lee hires the kitchen staff and has little difficulty in retaining them. He rules the kitchen when he is there (Sam does when he is not) and the managers and owners do not interfere with him. The only person who has ever been able to tell him what to do is Sam Jones. However, Sam has such respect for Charlie that he almost never overrules his decisions. Sam and Charlie often have lunch together in the afternoons in the kitchen with the rest of the kitchen staff.

Jean Jones decided that an assistant manager was needed about 20 years ago, and a woman named Sarah Smith was hired. Since then, Sarah has gradually taken complete charge of the restaurant and the staff except for the kitchen. Sarah and Charlie Lee did not get along very well for several years because Sarah made the mistake of interfering in Charlie's kitchen on her first day. Charlie chased her out of the kitchen and told her not to come back. Now each has accepted the jurisdiction of the other and they work very well together. Although neither will ever admit it publicly, they have developed a genuine admiration for each other.

The restaurant has a business manager named Paul Laberge, an accountant. Paul was hired 15 years ago to manage the financial affairs and he now has complete knowledge of the operations and financial affairs to a greater extent than anyone else, even Sam or Jean Jones. Paul stays in the background and is virtually unknown to the customers.

The manager of the bar and lounge is Louis Roy. He has been with the operation for 20 years and has complete responsibility for the purchase and sale of alcoholic beverages. Louis is Paul Laberge's uncle and it was Louis who suggested that Paul be hired. Although Sam and Jean had doubts at the time, they hired Paul out of respect for Louis. It has proved to be one of their more astute moves because Paul has helped to reduce costs and increase profits to such a great extent that he more than compensates for his salary. For the last 5 years, Louis has had health and personal problems that have reduced his effectiveness, but he has been kept on staff because his nephew has covered for him and because he is considered part of the family.

The waiters, waitresses, busboys and chefs (about 80 people) are hired as needed by either Charlie, Sarah or Paul, depending on the position. Many of these employees remain for many years and some have been with the restaurant almost as long as Jean and Sam. Although Sam and Jean could hire and fire the staff themselves, they prefer to let the others do it.

Ownership

Sam Jones owns a company called SJ Enterprises Limited which owns the restaurant, the land and the office buildings. Sam and Jean Jones jointly own SJJ Limited which owns the apartment building and other rental properties. Jones Farms Limited owns the farm and Sam plans to have it own his home in Florida. Jones Farms Limited is owned by SJ Enterprises Limited and SJJ Limited in proportions of 1/3 and 2/3 respectively.

The actual wealth of Sam and Jean Jones is something that has not been exactly calculated. Sam thinks that it is several million dollars, but he is not sure. Paul Laberge has provided the financial statements of the restaurant, but the real estate values of the farm, the apartments and the office buildings have not been calculated since acquisition. Dates of acquisition are from 5 to 25 years ago, and the purchase prices are, therefore, inaccurate estimates of current value. Paul Laberge and Sam's children have been urging Sam and Jean to obtain an up-to-date valuation, but nothing has yet been done about it. Prices paid at purchase and current indebtedness (mortgages) outstanding are found in Exhibit I.

FINANCIAL HISTORY

The initial financing of the restaurant occurred in 1958 with a $40,000 loan from the Antarctic Bank and an equal amount from the partners. Security for the loan was a first mortgage on the restaurant. This loan was the beginning of a thirty-year relationship between the lender and the restaurant.

Over the succeeding years the loans gradually increased. First there was expansion of the facilities, then there was purchase of additional land, followed by purchase of some of the partners ownership interests. The loans, by the end of 10 years, had reached $250,000, still secured by a first mortgage on buildings, land and chattels.

During the next decade, Sam Jones acquired the land and buildings adjacent to his restaurant, including the office building. The restaurant was also expanded to its current capacity. Indebtedness increased to $550,000 by 1978 and the security for the loans was enhanced to include the additional real estate.

In recent years, the restaurant has been remodelled and upgraded to its present decor. The last partnership interests were also acquired. The total indebtedness has not increased substantially, and it is now $800,000. Other debts of the Jones's are not part of the restaurant financial statements.

Financial statements for Jean's Place for the years from 1978 to 1987 are found in Exhibits II and III. These statements disclose the financial status of the company over the last few years. Sales have been fairly steadily increasing over the decade, but income has not been as stable, and losses occurred in the early 1980's. Assets and liabilities also show increases over the decade but they increase in lumps not in a gradual manner. More detailed study of the financial statements has not been done by Paul Laberge at this time.

VALUATION OF THE FIRM AND FINANCIAL PLANNING

There has been no attempt to value Jean's Place since the agreement to buy out the partners was established a number of years ago. That agreement did not provide a market value but rather it was based upon the partnership agreement signed some 30 years ago. In the partnership agreement book value plus cumulative profit share was the price for acquisition of a partner's share unless otherwise agreed by all partners. Sam's purchase of his partners' interests had been carried out using this method because they could not agree on an alternative.

Sam and Jean Jones want to value the restaurant in preparation for sale prior to retirement. They have talked to Paul Laberge (their accountant) and he has suggested a number of valuation techniques including book value, liquidation value, real estate value and going-concern value. He discussed several going-concern valuation techniques based upon cash flows and profits, but Sam and Jean did not fully understand them.

The other assets of Sam and Jean Jones are primarily real estate holdings and they feel that appraisals will provide a reasonable value. They are uncertain about when to sell and what to sell, with respect to the real estate, to facilitate their retirement.

Sam and Jean have accumulated Registered Retirement Savings Plans for themselves and their present values are $75,000 and $50,000 respectively. They are not sure about the adequacy of these funds for their retirement. Paul Laberge has suggested that they speak to a financial planner to help them ensure the adequacy of the amounts in the retirement funds and make appropriate financial plans for the future.

A search for prospective purchasers for the restaurant is an issue that the present owners have been thinking about very seriously. They see a number of possible options. The existing management could buy them out in some form of leveraged buyout arrangement. These people would probably only have a small amount of capital to make a down-payment, but the profits would probably pay the debt given enough time.

The owner could seek an outside buyer for his restaurant. This would probably be a cleaner arrangement and it would provide the cash more quickly. There is a risk that the present managers and staff would not be protected if such a buyout occurred.

© John Wiley Sons Canada Ltd. All rights reserved.

The final option for Sam Jones is to offer his children the opportunity to buy him out. This seems to be a remote possibility at the present, but Sam has always secretly hoped to pass his business on to his children. He has not given up on the idea completely.

TAX IMPLICATIONS

Sam Jones and Paul Laberge have talked a great deal about tax minimization in the event of a sale of the business or the real estate or both. Neither Sam nor Paul is a tax expert, but Sam has not been willing to consult someone else for help. Paul believes that the time has come to get expert advice. He has offered to arrange it, but Sam is still reluctant. Sam feels that he would be spending too much money on the tax specialist for the benefit that he would receive.

The discussions with the tax specialist would require that Sam and Jean prepare detailed financial plans and information. This they have not done either. Sam seems reluctant to share his personal financial information with an outsider.

OTHER FUTURE PLANS

Sam and Jean Jones believe that the restaurant will need a major face-lift soon. Both the inside and the outside will need to be upgraded within 2 or 3 years. The expense involved will exceed $500,000 and neither Sam nor Jean really wants to go through the renovation process again. More than anything else, this has caused the serious discussions about retirement from the restaurant and possible sale of the business.

Sam and Jean want to provide for their children and for their employees because they consider them all to be family. This overriding concern for these people will affect their decisions about the sale of their business and their other real estate. It will affect the timing of the decisions and the financing that will be acceptable.

CASE REQUIREMENT

Sam and Jean Jones need a comprehensive business and financial plan, based upon expert financial and tax advice, which provides several alternatives and their respective consequences. Careful consideration must be given to the objectives that Sam and Jean Jones have articulated or suggested. Paul Laberge will co-operate with you to provide any financial information that he can, as will Sam and Jean.

Play the role of the consultant who has been hired to give this advice.

EXHIBIT I
JEAN'S PLACE
INFORMATION ON REAL ESTATE HOLDINGS
(in dollars)

Date	Description	Purchase Price	Mortgage Outstanding
31-3-68	Office Building and Parking	250,000	50,000
30-6-64	House	40,000	-0-
30-9-72	Apartments	400,000	100,000
31-1-74	Duplex	85,000	10,000
31-10-78	Fourplex	150,000	50,000
31-5-80	Apartments	240,000	150,000
30-4-82	Farm	350,000	210,000
Total		1,515,000	570,000

EXHIBIT II
JEAN'S PLACE
INCOME STATEMENTS (in $000)

	1978	1979	1980	1981	1982	1983	1984	1985	1986	1987
Sales	1,680	1,848	2,070	2,882	3,148	2,760	2,834	3,118	2,987	2,733
Cost of Goods Sold	660	774	856	1,177	1,211	1,134	1,200	1,261	1,247	1,143
Gross Operating Profit	1,020	1,074	1,214	1,705	1,937	1,626	1,634	1,857	1,740	1,590
Selling Expenses										
Labour	347	400	457	635	753	724	761	770	763	689
Supplies	17	19	21	26	32	20	28	27	26	26
Advertising	12	14	14	14	14	16	13	9	10	10
Uniforms & Cleaning	14	12	14	19	21	17	17	18	16	16
Utilities	13	14	17	30	36	39	44	47	46	46
General	21	18	17	39	21	61	65	67	76	76
Franchise Fees	24	25	36	46	46	41	42	46	43	43
Travel & Auto	13	14	13	15	20	24	23	27	17	20
Total Selling Expenses	461	516	589	824	943	942	933	1,011	997	926

© John Wiley Sons Canada Ltd. All rights reserved.

EXHIBIT II (continued)
JEAN'S PLACE
INCOME STATEMENTS (in $000)

	1978	1979	1980	1981	1982	1983	1984	1985	1986	1987
Administrative & Financial Expenses										
Management & Office Salaries	80	80	80	80	470	296	196	327	1	61
Professional Fees	8	7	4	9	7	9	7	5	21	10
Telephone	3	3	2	4	4	5	6	7	6	6
Insurance & Taxes	23	24	26	32	43	49	52	53	56	60
Repairs & Maintneance	41	46	48	81	102	63	78	61	65	65
Menus & Signs	7	6	2	6	4	4	2	3	4	4
General	2	6	8	9	11	14	14	8	7	7
Depreciation	40	43	41	172	154	150	165	147	131	133
Interest & Bank Charges	54	31	38	190	202	147	192	167	146	133
Misc.	3	4	4	4	1	2	2	2	2	2
Total Administrative & Financial Expenses	261	250	253	587	998	739	714	780	439	481
Total Selling, Administrative & Financial Expenses	722	766	842	1,411	1,941	1,681	1,647	1,791	1,436	1,407
Operating Profit Before Taxes	298	308	372	294	(4)	(55)	(13)	66	304	183
Taxes	138	143	175	145	nil	nil	nil	nil	110	67
Net Profit or Loss	160	165	197	149	(4)	(55)	(13)	66	194	116
Dividends Paid	150	95	85	80	85	35	25	25	50	75
Addition to Retained Earnings	10	70	112	69	(89)	(90)	(38)	41	144	41

© John Wiley Sons Canada Ltd. All rights reserved.

EXHIBIT III
JEAN'S PLACE
BALANCE SHEETS (in $000)

	1978	1979	1980	1981	1982	1983	1984	1985	1986	1987
Current Assets										
Cash	156	167	35	94	219	249	108	289	175	65
Accounts Receivable	14	14	25	33	40	130	44	41	39	31
Quick Assets	170	181	60	127	259	379	152	330	214	96
Inventories	47	52	67	76	92	73	71	93	98	80
Prepaid Expenses	10	27	22	38	29	7	8	6	6	42
Total Current Assets	227	260	149	241	380	459	231	429	318	218
Fixed Assets										
Land	171	171	171	171	171	567	496	496	496	496
Buildings	291	317	680	1,230	1,335	1,546	1,762	1,771	1,771	1,771
Less Reserve for Depreciation	138	156	175	268	392	496	614	728	813	871
Vehicles	14	25	32	32	32	32	42	42	42	42
Less Reserve for Depreciation	5	13	18	22	26	27	30	34	36	37
Furniture & Fixtures	229	249	340	463	465	488	555	574	574	574
Reserve for Depreciation	147	168	180	232	284	322	370	418	441	455
Paving	8	8	20	20	20	20	20	20	20	20
Reserve for Depreciation	2	3	6	4	5	6	7	8	9	10
Total Fixed Assets Net of Depreciation	421	430	864	1,390	1,316	1,802	1,854	1,715	1,604	1,530
Other Assets										
Loans Receivable from Employees	163	156	274	273	253	154	53	-0-	-0-	59
Total Assets	811	846	1,287	1,904	1,949	2,415	2,138	2,144	1,922	1,807

© John Wiley Sons Canada Ltd. All rights reserved.

EXHIBIT III (continued)
JEAN'S PLACE
BALANCE SHEETS (IN $000)

	1978	1979	1980	1981	1982	1983	1984	1985	1986	1987
Current Liabilities										
Bank Loans, Overdraft & Outstanding Cheques	-0-	-0-	-0-	-0-	-0-	-0-	-0-	78	-0-	38
Accounts Payable	60	65	222	114	70	53	95	119	90	66
Accrued Expenses	21	21	30	48	30	159	352	355	169	115
Tax Liability	91	76	141	143	23	-0-	-0-	23	102	-0-
Current Bank Instalments	20	25	25	42	42	47	86	90	111	128
Total Current Liabilities	192	187	418	347	165	259	533	665	472	347
Deferred Liabilities										
Bank Loan (Total)	218	198	196	882	840	1,093	1,046	960	870	932
Less Current Instalments	20	25	25	42	42	47	86	90	111	128
Loans from Shareholders	30	25	122	72	430	644	217	140	78	2
Total Deferred Liabilities	228	198	293	912	1,228	1,690	1,177	1,010	837	806
Net Worth										
Share Capital	3	3	3	3	3	3	3	3	3	3
Retained Earnings	388	458	573	642	553	463	425	466	610	651
Total Net Worth	391	461	576	645	556	466	428	469	613	654
Total Liabilities & Net Worth	811	846	1,287	1,904	1,949	2,415	2,138	2,144	1,922	1,807

CASE 15

UNIVERSITY OF WASHINGTON OVERHEAD CHARGES

E. Noreen
University of Washington
Seattle, Washington

The University of Washington is a large (32,000 enrolment) teaching and research institution located in Seattle, Washington. The University is supported by funds provided by the state of Washington, by grants and contracts, and by certain fee revenues. The University is not directly supported by the tuition that is charged to its regularly enrolled students, which goes into the state's general fund.

Prior to 1982, overhead costs at the University (e.g., physical plant support services, central administration, personnel support, etc.) were charged to units of the University on a fee-for-services-provided basis. For example, the parking division was charged for the cost of periodically repainting parking spaces. However, under this policy much of the overhead of the University had not been charged to any operating unit. For example, since it was difficult to identify the services provided by the President's office, those costs had not been assigned to any operating unit of the University.

A recession — which particularly affected the lumber industry in the state of Washington — resulted in several budget crises at the University between 1979 and 1984. The budget provided by the state for the 1979-1981 biennium had been cut five percent below the level of the previous biennium and the budget for the 1982-1983 biennium was reduced a further 5.5% below that level. These financial difficulties prompted a review of the University's policy for recovering overhead costs, and a consultant was hired in November of 1982 to determine the implicit subsidies to certain University programs as a result of incomplete recovery of overhead costs.

Based on the results of that cost study, the Provost of the University, George Beckman, informed the heads of certain units that the fees charged for their programs — and perhaps the programs themselves — might be called into question. The methods used in the cost study were explained to the heads of University units in a letter dated October 11, 1983, signed by Robert Thompson, the Vice Provost for Planning and Budgeting. A copy of the letter, sent to Nancy Jacob, Dean of the School of Business Administration, is included as Appendix A to this case.

The letter from the Vice Provost mentions that a charge of between three and five percent of revenues would go into effect January 1, 1984 — basically, an "across-the-board" tax. Funds generated by this overhead charge would be used to finance the central administrative structure of the University. Such services as admissions, registration, library resources and computer services would be subsidized by this "tax." The budget committee would make the decision each year as to where the funds will be spent. Applications from the various academic units would also be considered for supplementary funding above the normal budget. These would be prioritized by the budget committee and funded up to the limits of the available funds.

After meeting with many of the heads of revenue-producing departments affected by the proposed overhead charge, the Provost modified his plans and informed units in a letter sent out on January 26, 1984. A copy of that letter, with its attachments, is included in this case as Appendix B. Attachment II to the letter indicates that the overhead rate would be 8.1% of revenues in the 1983-85 biennium rather than three to five percent as previously announced. In Attachment III to the letter, units are advised to increase their fees by 8.81% to maintain their revenues at pre-overhead charge levels.

The major University fee-generating programs that would be affected by the overhead charges are listed in Appendix C.

CASE REQUIREMENTS

1. Was an across-the-board surcharge to self-sustaining and revenue-generating programs the only alternative for the Administration to take? What other alternatives might there have been? What would be the advantages and disadvantages of each?

2. The October 11, 1983 letter indicated that the overhead rate would be in the three to five percent range. Why did the overhead rate ultimately turn out to be 8.1% instead?

3. What advice would you give the Provost concerning cross-subsidization of programs and how fees should be adjusted?

4. The overhead charge system is, as the case says, a tax. How equitable is such a tax? What does it accomplish?

5. Some programs and services are charged different rates or no surcharge at all. Does this improve the fairness of the system? Why or why not?

APPENDIX A
UNIVERSITY OF WASHINGTON OVERHEAD CHARGES
LETTER OF OCTOBER 11, 1983

University Of Washington
Seattle, Washington 98195

October 11, 1983

Nancy L. Jacob, Dean
School of Business Administration DJ-10

Dear Dean Jacob:

This letter is to follow up Dr. Beckman's letter of September 23, 1983 to provide additional information on the recently completed University study of overhead costs. The study was designed to identify the cost of providing University support services to all University programs and activities, including self-sustaining and other revenue generating units. It was commissioned by the University Budget Committee (UBC) in November, 1982 to provide a basis for reviewing subsidies to self-sustaining and revenue generating units and for considering possible implementation of new cost recovery policies. The review was conducted by the Planning and Budgeting Office with the aid of an outside consultant.

The study was completed early last May and has since undergone a good deal of review by the UBC, which approved the concept of applying an overhead surcharge to cash revenue in self-sustaining and other revenue generating programs. The 1983-85 biennium operating budget was formulated with the assumption that an additional $2.0 million will be realized from this source. The target date for implementing the surcharge is January 1, 1984. Accordingly, you should be planning now on the assumption that an initial surcharge of between three and five percent will go into effect January 1, 1984.

A three to five percent overhead rate will recover only a small portion of the overhead costs incurred by University budgets on behalf of self-sustaining and revenue generating units as measured by the cost study. The $2.0 million to be charged thus represents a modest initial implementation of a new overhead cost recovery policy for the University.

Thank you for your cooperation.

Sincerely yours,

Robert K. Thompson
Vice Provost for Planning and Budgeting
Planning and Budgeting

Attachments

APPENDIX A — ATTACHMENT I
UNIVERSITY OF WASHINGTON OVERHEAD CHARGES
LETTER OF OCTOBER 11, 1983
Institutional Overhead Cost Study
Summary of Process

The initial step of the study was to gather financial and other data from University records. The Financial Accounting System (FAS) was a primary source of information. Fiscal 1981-82 expenditures and revenues, salaries and wages by sub-object, FTE's and CTI's, equipment expenditures and other operating costs were extracted from FAS by budget number.

The room inventory was used to obtain information about assigned square feet by organization. Information about building costs and about types of services provided in each building (fuel, electricity, water, janitorial, etc.) was obtained from the records of the Physical Plant office. The equipment inventory file was used for information about source and costs of equipment.

Faculty Activity Analysis (FAA) reports for academic year 1981-82 were the source of information about faculty time devoted to instruction, research, and university/college/department administration. Finally, instructional data were obtained from tenth-day enrolment files for Autumn Quarter 1982, specifically student credit hours (SCH) by department.

These dates were arranged, after necessary adjustments, by organization using the organization code structure within each program category (P/C). The principal adjustment involved modifying total expenditures to back out indirect cost charges and equipment purchases over $500 and to add in benefits and equipment use cost. The result, modified total direct costs or MTDC, was a major parameter in subsequent allocations of total university overhead costs. The space information also required adjustments to ensure that square footage was properly assigned by unit and in relation to central services supplied to the space.

The allocation of costs was done using software developed by the National Centre for Higher Education Management Systems. The allocation system involved a process in which costs of one overhead type (plant operations, for instance) were distributed on the basis of some parameter (square feet, in this case) to all benefiting units. Then, the next overhead cost (accounting, for example), including the overhead costs already allocated to it, was allocated (on the basis of MTDC in this case) to all units benefiting from the service. This step-down process or model resulted ultimately in the assignment of all the costs of all overhead units (sending accounts) to the group of all final cost programs or units (receiving accounts). (See Chart 1.) Table I summarizes the sending account costs to be allocated, while Table II summarizes the overhead costs allocated to each program or unit.

APPENDIX A — ATTACHEMENT II
UNIVERSITY OF WASHINGTON OVERHEAD CHARGES
LETTER OF OCTOBER 11, 1983
Institutional Overhead Cost Study
Summary of Process (continued)

The main parameters or measures which staff used as the basis for allocating support costs were square feet by type of service, MTDC, salaries and wages, FTE faculty and SCH. More specifically, major support cost groups were distributed on the following bases:

COST	PARAMETER
Capital	Square Feet
Plant Operations	Square Feet
Classroom Maintenance	FTE Faculty
Executive Management	MTDC
Support Services	MTDC
Student Services	SCH
Libraries	FTE Faculty
Department Administration	MTDC

The capital costs were derived from original building costs as identified in the Physical Plant report "Annual Building Maintenance Cost and Square Feet." For each building, a use allowance of two percent was calculated and allocated to each room based on its square footage. This use allowance was assigned to the organization using the room and appears as a building use cost.

The final result of running the allocation model was a set of allocated overhead cost for each unit within each P/C (each receiving account, in other words). The organizational summaries which are shown in Table II and which appear as the individual rate reports, are available from the allocation software routines.

The rate reports must be viewed with several caveats in mind: first, they are based on numbers which now will be subject to the scrutiny of the organization to which they relate. Second, the results do not reflect any overhead costs which some organizations may already bear through current indirect cost rates or through payment (CTI's) to some overhead (sending account) departments or units for services.

Finally, there is no allowance in the rate reports for legal or other official constraints on payment of institutional overhead costs, nor are there any provisions for marketplace concerns or for the relationship of unit's activities to the central mission of the University. All of these factors will be considered in any final decisions about overhead charges to individual units and should be documented.

APPENDIX A — ATTACHMENT III
UNIVERSITY OF WASHINGTON
LETTER OF OCTOBER 11, 1983
Chart I
Cost Accounting System
Implementation Flowchart
Fiscal Year 1982

SEQUENCE   **FLOW**

1. Plant operations and maintenance costs, P/C 091 through 093.

2. Classroom maintenance costs, P/C 018.

3. Institutional support costs, P/C 081 through 087.

4. Student service costs, P/C 061 through 063.

5. Library costs, P/C 051 and 052.

6. Academic administration and computer support costs, P/C 043 and 041.

7. Departmental administration costs, P/C 044.

8. Final cost objectives.

© John Wiley & Sons Canada Ltd. All rights reserved.

APPENDIX A — ATTACHMENT IV
LETTER OF OCTOBER 11, 1983
TABLE I
UNIVERSITY OF WASHINGTON
Indirect Cost Study Distribution Detail (in Dollars)

Support Program/Unit	Direct Costs	Bldg/Lease Allowance	Equipment Costs	Indirect Costs	Total Costs
Buildings & Grounds					
(P/C 092)	866,042	-0-	8,601	-0-	874,643
Grounds (P/C 092)					
To Sending Accounts					250,007
To Receiving Accounts					624,636
Total Allocation					874,643
Physical Plant Support Services (P/C 093)					
PP&C Design & Office Relocate	596,505	731	133	-0-	597,369
Administration & Engineering. Services & HS Expenses	1,155,089	4,942	7,104	-0-	1,167,135
Physical Plant Maintenance	-0-	-0-	769	-0-	769
Energy Management	400,665	-0-	1,059	-0-	401,724
Trucking Services	974,410	-0-	1,558	-0-	975,968
Fire Prevention	141,398	-0-	-0-	-0-	141,398
University Police	2,204,455	2,116	10,074	-0-	2,216,645
Environmental Health	801,995	3,574	3,765	-0-	809,334
Sub-Total	6,274,517	11,363	24,462	-0-	6,310,342
To Sending Accounts					1,373,006
To Receiving Accounts					4,737,336
Total Allocation					6,310,342
Executive Management (P/C 081)					
President	592,613	11,241	5,017	23,293	632,164
Provost	540,013	5,571	1,603	31,176	578,363
VP Planning & Budgeting	166,080	2,369	243	13,655	182,347
VP Business & Finance	250,867	633	976	3,646	256,122
VP University Relations	225,620	1,303	389	7,512	234,824
VP Research/Dean of Graduate School	108,102	-0-	438	-0-	108,540
VP Health Services	541,256	9,223	24,940	28,734	604,153
VP Computing (24%) (P/C 041)	1,439	-0-	133	-0-	1,572
Provost Computing Subsidy (P/C 041)	493,702	421	1,039	2,424	497,586
Sub-Total	2,919,692	30,761	34,778	110,440	3,095,671
To Sending Accounts					662,443
To Receiving Accounts					2,433,228
Total Allocation					3,095,671

APPENDIX A — ATTACHMENT IV
TABLE I (continued)

Support Program/Unit	Direct Costs	Bldg/Lease Allowance	Equipment Costs	Indirect Costs	Total Costs
Fiscal Services (P/C 082)					
Budget Office	370,876	2,145	-0-	12,364	383,385
Financial Services	366,507	1,919	456	11,138	380,020
General Accounting	921,774	4,229	2,171	8,593	936,767
Grant & Contract Accounting	743,986	2,307	427	4,688	751,408
Receivables Control	147,330	391	101	2,062	149,884
Cashiers Office	455,475	4,784	2,3724	22,360	484,991
Student Loans	394,840	3,085	442	14,417	412,784
Payroll Office	467,691	2,675	1,759	14,113	486,238
Equipment Inventory	83,600	20	-0-	146	83,766
Internal Audit	503,383	20,294	96	-0-	523,773
Sub-Total	4,455,462	41,849	7,824	89,881	4,595,016
To Sending Accounts					426,016
To Receiving Accounts					4,169,000
Total Allocation					4,595,016
Support Services (P/C 083)					
Attorney General	362,667	2,056	2,454	11,848	379,025
Provost	141,303	2,250	350	18,080	161,983
University Committees	167,271	1,563	129	9,009	177,972
Ombudsman	87,072	434	-0-	749	88,255
Equal Employment Office	439,432	2,513	856	16,554	459,355
Planning Studies	245,642	1,319	359	7,601	254,921
Capital Budget	114,046	504	354	2,906	117,810
VP Business & Finance	489,577	188	-0-	1,083	490,848
Business Services	149,641	1,280	43	7,377	158,341
Facilities Planning	940,215	1,852	343	22,653	965,063
Office Systems	73,683	-0-	1,492	-0-	75,175
Risk Management	2,907,694	356	110	2,053	2,910,213
Personnel Services	467,099	453	-0-	2,608	470,160
Staff Personnel	528,370	3,626	1,255	3,298	536,549
Hospital Staff Personnel	286,203	829	-0-	4,084	291,116
Staff Employment	508,881	9,863	2,101	33,811	554,656
Retirement & Insurance	325,586	1,191	262	6,281	333,320
Administrative Data Processing	3,635,194	247,770	33,547	11,269	3,927,780

APPENDIX A — ATTACHMENT IV
TABLE I(continued)

Support Program/Unit	Direct Costs	Bldg/Lease Allowance	Equipment Costs	Indirect Costs	Total Costs
Admissions & Records	103,254	-0-	1,583	-0-	104,837
VP University Relations	206,133	-0-	195	-0-	206,328
VP Research/Dean of Graduate School	543,288	2,932	648	16,902	563,770
VP University Relations —Development (P/C 085)	1,026,224	14,024	568	30,741	1,079,557
Graduate Support Services (P/C 085)	224,631	-0-	177	-0-	224,808
KCTS Management (P/C 085)	67,453	-0-	-0-	-0-	67,453
Health Sciences Information Centre (P/C 085)	166,959	917	783	4,516	173,175
Sub-Total	14,207,518	295,920	47,609	221,423	14,772,470
To Sending Accounts					1,645,592
To Receiving Accounts					13,126,878
Total Allocation					14,773,470
Logistical Services (P/C 084)					
Communications Services	100,135	17,096	211	14,213	131,655
Campus Mail Services	2,803,676	1,623	9,588	8,431	2,823,318
Telecommunications	5,569,774	5,963	3,216	11,140	5,590,093
Purchasing	1,468,647	6,814	5,911	15,654	1,497,026
Equipment Inventory	128,908	62	274	453	129,697
Sub-Total	10,071,140	31,558	19,200	49,891	10,171,789
To Sending Accounts					1,196,877
To Receiving Accounts					8,974,912
Total Allocation					10,171,789
University Administration from Departments (FA4)	1,118,756	12,687	-0-	63,517	1,194,960
To Sending Accounts					140,611
To Receiving Accounts					1,054,349
Total Allocation					1,194,960
TOTAL	39,913,127	424,138	142,474	535,152	41,014,891
To Sending Accounts					5,894,552
To Receiving Accounts					35,120,339
Total Allocation					41,014,891

APPENDIX A — ATTACHMENT V
LETTER OF OCTOBER 11, 1983
TABLE II
UNIVERSITY OF WASHINGTON
Indirect Cost Study Distribution

Program/Organizations	M T D C	Capital	Unadjusted Plant	Distribution Class Maint.	Admin.
ADP Self-Sustaining	862,120	-0-	387	-0-	55,492
Animal Medicine	1,592,857	40,563	116,204	761	111,321
Applied Physics Laboratory	13,135,211	30,942	282,261	-0-	999,272
Associated University Physicians	3,091,379	-0-	-0-	-0-	198,984
Central Stores	5,994,801	28,388	236,033	-0-	385,865
Chargeable Shops	4,085,988	33,973	176,656	-0-	263,002
Continuing Education	3,184,665	4,359	43,672	2,465	207,170
Dental Clinic	1,866,997	85,470	282,468	-0-	128,427
Education Assessment Centre	385,691	6,703	31,325	-0-	25,831
Fisheries Vessels	469,752	-0-	-0-	-0-	30,236
Friday Harbour Laboratory & House	198,748	37,626	217,992	-0-	12,963
Hall Health & Vision	1,856,136	55,460	68,516	-0-	119,472
Harbourview Hospital	43,021,947	-0-	338,856	-0-	2,860,436
Health Sciences Stores	8,946,350	44,494	144,532	-0-	575,846
Henry Art Gallery	262,078	5,849	48,631	-0-	16,988
Housing/Food Administration	1,125,985	12,082	34,555	-0-	72,476
ICA Sports Facilities	672,982	204,788	401,897	-0-	43,318
Intercollegiate Athletics	5,408,309	17,921	71,810	-0-	352,559
ICGS — Richland	2,587,603	45,065	555	-0-	191,464

APPENDIX A — ATTACHMENT V
LETTER OF OCTOBER 11, 1983
TABLE II
UNIVERSITY OF WASHINGTON
Indirect Cost Study Distribution

Students	Libraries	Acad. Support	Dept. Admin.	Total	Rate(%)
		Unadjusted	Distribution		
-0-	-0-	-0-	-0-	55,879	6.48
-0-	20,645	15,995	89,024	394,513	24.77
-0-	12,942	53,022	29,960	1,408,399	10.72
-0-	-0-	31,043	-0-	230,027	7.44
-0-	-0-	-0-	-0-	650,286	10.85
-0-	-0-	-0-	-0-	473,631	11.59
-0-	7,227	408,549	8,435	681,877	21.41
-0-	-0-	135,830	-0-	632,195	33.86
-0-	-0-	152	-0-	64,011	16.60
-0-	-0-	13,760	-0-	43,996	9.37
-0-	-0-	11,632	264,580	544,793	274.11
-0-	-0-	-0-	-0-	243,448	13.12
-0-	643	-0-	-0-	3,199,935	7.44
-0-	-0-	-0-	-0-	764,872	8.55
-0-	-0-	3,257	-0-	74,725	28.51
-0-	-0-	-0-	-0-	119,113	10.58
-0-	-0-	-0-	-0-	650,003	96.59
-0-	-0-	-0-	-0-	442,290	8.18
-0-	25,914	752	-0-	263,750	10.19

APPENDIX A — ATTACHMENT V
TABLE II (continued)

Program/Organizations	MTDC	Capital	Unadjusted Plant	Distribution Class Maint.	Admin.
John Locke Computer Centre	791,559	5,403	12,569	-0-	54,450
KCTS Television	4,031,823	19,481	97,618	-0-	336,614
KUOW/KCMU Radio	396,641	2,457	24,241	-0-	28,750
Medicine — FHCRC	221,714	-0-	-0-	-0-	16,863
Medicine — HMC	3,683,840	-0-	-0-	-0-	268,121
Medicine — PHS	1,685,099	71,006	-0-	-0-	128,136
Medicine — Providence	379,378	-0-	-0-	-0-	28,878
Medicine — Van	321,250	10,454	-0-	-0-	24,407
Motorpool	1,065,721	8,288	34,152	-0-	68,598
Museum	698,456	32,035	279,493	-0-	46,106
Mack Forest	279,806	9,487	30,721	-0-	18,008
Packing Division	1,912,468	229,422	806,293	-0-	123,100
Primate Centre	2,992,318	37,734	310,725	-0-	227,746
Public Performing Arts	864,660	99,665	256,112	-0-	55,655
Printing Plant	6,778,095	24,273	161,193	-0-	436,282
Recreational Sports	1,113,513	128,497	375,458	-0-	71,673
Residental Halls/Family House	8,974,640	733,898	2,280,750	-0-	577,665
Retail Food Service	4,463,701	112,008	248,474	-0-	287,313
South Campus Centre	174,528	14,528	58,979	-0-	11,234
Student Publications	632,669	2,016	15,407	-0-	40,721
Student Union Building	1,802,727	72,307	386,998	-0-	116,035
University Hospital	59,923,601	808,551	859,281	-0-	3,984,548
University Press	1,692,759	7,982	19,367	-0-	109,212
General University Instruction	52,584,670	672,943	3,901,691	1,664,985	3,619,578
Health Science Instruction	19,565,147	204,763	694,619	171,261	1,378,495
Auxiliary Education Actual — Campus	4,309,468	50,178	105,791	2,764	279,937
Auxiliary Education Actual — HS	16,254,308	348	6,402	221,168	1,055,863
Institutes & Residential Centres	2,132,246	20,029	85,887	-0-	163,057
Individual Project Research	387,321	-0-	-0-	-0-	26,717
Community Services	251,256	13,156	60,472	-0-	16,172
Ancillary Supply Services	1,817,938	39,334	118,808	-0-	117,003

APPENDIX A — ATTACHMENT V
TABLE II (continued)

Students	Libraries	Unadjusted Distribution		Total	Rate(%)
		Acad. Support	Dept. Admin.		
-0-	-0-	7,949	45,894	126,265	15.95
-0-	-0-	-0-	-0-	453,713	11.25
-0-	-0-	-0-	-0-	55,448	13.98
-0-	3,007	2,226	-0-	22,096	9.97
-0-	82,621	37,075	-0-	387,817	10.53
-0-	36,056	17,141	-0-	252,339	14.97
-0-	9,715	3,810	-0-	42,403	11.18
-0-	9,969	3,455	-0-	48,285	15.03
-0-	-0-	-0-	-0-	111,038	10.42
-0-	15,947	8,679	-0-	382,260	54.73
-0-	-0-	13,932	-0-	72,148	25.79
-0-	-0-	-0-	-0-	1,158,815	60.59
-0-	19,888	-0-	-0-	596,093	19.92
-0-	-0-	12,268	77,032	500,732	57.91
-0-	-0-	-0-	-0-	621,748	9.17
-0-	-0-	-0-	-0-	575,628	51.69
-0-	-0-	-0-	-0-	3,592,313	40.03
-0-	-0-	-0-	-0-	647,795	14.51
-0-	-0-	-0-	-0-	84,741	48.55
-0-	-0-	-0-	-0-	58,144	9.19
-0-	94,490	-0-	-0-	669,830	37.16
-0-	585	-0-	-0-	5,652,965	9.43
-0-	-0-	99,068	-0-	235,629	13.92
6,894,238	6,098,001	3,875,718	15,932,877	42,660,031	81.13
641,524	3,172,799	850,393	4,221,762	11,335,616	57.94
-0-	8,098	46,941	187,933	681,642	15.82
-0-	2,530,994	227,731	1,102,378	5,144,884	31.65
-0-	134,454	80,430	74,353	558,210	26.18
-0-	9,110	27,953	36,889	100,669	25.99
-0-	4,021	8,314	71,265	173,400	69.01
-0-	22,189	73,961	86,419	457,714	25.18

© John Wiley & Sons Canada Ltd. All rights reserved.

APPENDIX A
TABLE II (continued)

Program/ Organizations	M T D C	Capital	Unadjusted Plant	Distribution Class Maint.	Admin.
Federal On-Campus Research	48,840,454	820,172	3,690,759	-0-	3,718,260
Federal Off-Campus Research	18,423,462	642	17,301	-0-	1,402,591
Federal Training Grants	18,361,240	182,607	637,731	-0-	1,397,844
Federal Miscellaneous Research	2,250,800	22,723	94,924	-0-	171,345
Non-Federal On-Campus Research	11,758,709	151,702	695,433	-0-	886,185
Non-Federal Off-Campus Research	3,906,654	260	10,363	-0-	294,435
Non-Federal Training Grants	3,287,789	34,158	109,639	-0-	247,768
Non-Federal Miscellaneous Research	5,424,973	51,020	203,223	-0-	408,847
CETA	710	-0-	-0-	-0-	-0-
Outside Business	-0-	42,801	59,909	-0-	-0-
Unassigned Space	-0-	35,515	-0-	-0-	-0-
Service Operations	8,434,140	78,637	295,642	-0-	553,094
Auxiliary Enterprises	1,149,339	12,449	19,223	-0-	73,984
Agency/Suspense Accounts	3,665,864	23,156	114,227	-0-	235,955
CUMULATIVE TOTAL	426,437,053	5,539,768	19,676,225	2,063,404	29,758,367

APPENDIX A — ATTACHMENT V
TABLE II (continued)

Students	Libraries	Acad. Support	Unadjusted Distribution Dept. Admin.	Total	Rate(%)
-0-	1,537,059	879,316	7,206,887	17,852,453	36.55
-0-	328,979	432,499	1,654,099	3,836,111	20.82
-0-	649,146	623,256	3,279,844	6,770,428	36.87
-0-	89,220	48,339	185,858	612,409	27.21
-0-	312,018	254,077	1,567,678	3,867,093	32.89
-0-	99,298	120,962	468,577	993,895	25.44
-0-	94,279	135,762	487,068	1,108,674	33.72
-0-	109,412	153,610	800,380	1,726,492	31.82
-0-	-0-	-0-	-0-	-0-	-0-
-0-	-0-	-0-	-0-	102,710	-0-
-0-	-0-	-0-	-0-	35,515	-0-
-0-	81	128,151	1,329,823	2,385,428	28.28
-0-	-0-	3,924	103,824	213,404	18.57
-0-	159,403	32,917	405,912	971,570	26.50
7,535,762	15,698,210	8,883,849	39,718,751	128,874,336	30.22

APPENDIX B
UNIVERSITY OF WASHINGTON
LETTER OF JANUARY 26, 1984

University Of Washington
Seattle, Washington 98195

January 26, 1984

Deans
Vice-Presidents
Directors Of Libraries

Dear Colleagues:

At the beginning of the 1983-85 biennium, the University Budget Committee adopted the general policy to charge overhead costs to self-sustaining and revenue supported budgets. Attachment I summarizes the background for this decision and subsequent steps taken to consult with potentially affected units and develop a proposal. As a result of these deliberations, a specific policy proposal has been developed and reviewed by the University Budget Committee. A copy of this policy proposal is attached (II) along with a schedule showing the amounts to be recharged to your units according to this proposal. The purpose of this letter is to introduce the policy and to solicit your comments and input before the University Budget Committee adopts a policy and makes final implementation decisions.

The general policy is to charge all cash revenue accounts, with certain possible exceptions, a common University average overhead rate designed to recover overhead costs associated with building use, institutional support and plant operation and maintenance. The policy allows for rate adjustments in cases where some portion of this overhead base may not be appropriate for certain units. For example, units located off campus would not be charged for plant operation and maintenance costs and those occupying buildings purchased or constructed from non-state funds would not be charged for building use costs.

Let me remind you that the University needs to generate at least $2.0 million net of exemptions this biennium to balance our biennial budget. Units should not, therefore, assume that many exemptions (number and dollar volume) will be forthcoming except in truly exceptional cases with complete and convincing justification.

Sincerely yours,

George M. Beckman
Provost

APPENDIX B
UNIVERSITY OF WASHINGTON
LETTER OF JANUARY 26, 1984
Attachment I
University Institutional Overhead Policy
Background and Schedule

1. **Background**

   A. A cost study was conducted, starting in November 1982, by the Office of Planning and Budgeting team through a steering committee, using a consultant and drawing on the experience of a similar effort at Ohio State University.

   B. Cost study results were reviewed by the UBC in early Summer 1983 in conjunction with the 1983-85 budget allocation process. The UBC:

   • Reviewed various levels and distributions of overhead charges.

   • Recognized the largest impact would be on the Hospitals and because of the technical and policy complexities it was decided not to assume immediate implementation for Hospitals pending completion of the policy analysis.

2. **Subsequent Steps**

   The Provost met with the Directors of major auxiliary enterprises and revenue generating units in September 1983 to brief them on the underlying proposals and assumptions.

   Cost reports were distributed to the affected Schools and Colleges in October 1983.

   Meetings with unit administrators were held in November and early December to explain the Overhead Cost Study and to solicit comments and suggestions.

   Most frequent comments from units were variations on the theme "not us, we're special." Some campus organizations raised questions concerning the methodology of the cost study and policy questions about the application of overhead rates to specific organizations or types of organizations.

APPENDIX II
UNIVERSITY OF WASHINGTON
LETTER OF JANUARY 26, 1984
Attachment II
University Institutional Overhead Policy and Implementation Plan

1. **Policy**

   Overhead costs are a legitimate cost of conducting the business of the University. Failure to recognize and properly apportion overhead costs results in hidden subsidies to some programs. While the University may wish to subsidize certain programs as a matter of policy, these subsidy decisions should be explicit and considered in the biennial budget process.

   The basic policy will be to recover these costs by charging a University-wide average rate to all units. Following is a summary of the 1983-85 campus wide average rate for the three cost components:

Building Costs	1.34%
Plant Operations and Maintenance	4.86%
Institutional Support	<u>7.01%</u>
Total	13.21%

   This rate may be adjusted where it causes a serious inequity to the unit affected or the rate is clearly inappropriate.

2. **Implementation Plan**

   Implementation of this new policy will be phased in over the current and succeeding biennia as follows:

   1983-85 — Recover $2,000,000 above current amounts by charging 13.21% scaled down to 8.81% based on revenue received after January 1, 1984.

   1985-87 — Recover the full 13.21% (as updated).

   Amounts currently paid for overhead functions will continue to be paid but will be offset against general University overhead charges to the paying unit. Eventually most of these special payments will be discontinued because overhead rates will encompass the costs involved.

© John Wiley & Sons Canada Ltd. All rights reserved.

APPENDIX B
UNIVERSITY OF WASHINGTON
LETTER OF JANUARY 26, 1984
Attachment III
Overhead Cost Recovery Implementation Process

1. The Budget office has prepared a list of budgets to be charged and exempted. The list includes the specific rate to be charged or, in a very few cases, a specific dollar amount to be charged. The rates to be charged have been adjusted for pass-through and credits.

2. The General Accounting Office will use the list to prepare Journal Vouchers each quarter (starting with January – March 1984) to charge the appropriate budgets. The formula "Rate/(100 + Rate)" will be applied against revenue in the appropriate revenue codes (9402, 9420, 9424, 9430, 9499). For example, if a rate of 8.81% applies to a budget which earned $10,000 in revenue during the quarter (all in revenue code 9420) the charge would be $810. This is calculated as follows:

$$\frac{8.81}{100 + 8.81} = \frac{8.81}{108.81} \qquad .081(8.1\%) \times \$10{,}000 = \$810$$

There is often some confusion about the 8.81% rate and the 8.1% rate. The 8.81% is the average amount by which customers' bills must be increased to cover indirect or overhead costs. The 8.1% is the rate the General Accounting Office will apply to total revenue (regular revenue plus overhead charges) to subtract overhead amounts from the budgets which collect it.

3. The only action required of individual budget holders is to raise the rates charged to customers or otherwise accommodate the revenue charge which will be made according to the above process.

APPENDIX C
UNIVERSITY OF WASHINGTON
Significant Overhead Charges by Program
Estimates for the Remainder of the 1983 – 1985 Biennium
(in dollars)

	Revenue	Overhead Charges	Effective Rate
Audio Visual Services	265,000	17,503	8.81%
Computer Equipment Fund	157,200	10,383	8.81%
Printing Plant	1,665,600	93,773	7.51%
Parking	5,650,984	324,225	7.65%
Health Science Stores	1,600,000	105,680	8.81%
Food Services	11,278,800	563,122	6.66%
Wind Tunnel	1,275,334	51,741	5.41%
Museum Sales	492,024	32,498	8.81%
Continuing Education:			
General	6,262,108	100,000	2.13%
Business Administration	2,409,700	39,932	2.21%
Dentistry	1,205,388	39,808	4.40%
Medical	1,690,728	55,836	4.40%
Nursing	423,374	13,982	4.40%
Engineering	554,068	18,299	4.40%
Forest Resources	489,000	16,150	4.40%

INTEREST TABLES

Table 1 — Future Amount of 1

Table 2 — Present Value of 1

Table 3 — Future Amount of an Ordinary Annuity of 1 per Period

Table 4 — Present Value of an Ordinary Annuity of 1 per Period

Table 5 — Present Value of an Annuity Due of 1 per Period

TABLE 6-1 FUTURE AMOUNT OF 1 (Future Amount of a Single Sum)

$$a_{\overline{n}|i} = (1 + i)^n$$

(n) Periods	2%	2½%	3%	4%	5%	6%
1	1.02000	1.02500	1.03000	1.04000	1.05000	1.06000
2	1.04040	1.05063	1.06090	1.08160	1.10250	1.12360
3	1.06121	1.07689	1.09273	1.12486	1.15763	1.19102
4	1.08243	1.10381	1.12551	1.16986	1.21551	1.26248
5	1.10408	1.13141	1.15927	1.21665	1.27628	1.33823
6	1.12616	1.15969	1.19405	1.26532	1.34010	1.41852
7	1.14869	1.18869	1.22987	1.31593	1.40710	1.50363
8	1.17166	1.21840	1.26677	1.36857	1.47746	1.59385
9	1.19509	1.24886	1.30477	1.42331	1.55133	1.68948
10	1.21899	1.28008	1.34392	1.48024	1.62889	1.79085
11	1.24337	1.31209	1.38423	1.53945	1.71034	1.89830
12	1.26824	1.34489	1.42576	1.60103	1.79586	2.01220
13	1.29361	1.37851	1.46853	1.66507	1.88565	2.13293
14	1.31948	1.41297	1.51259	1.73168	1.97993	2.26090
15	1.34587	1.44830	1.55797	1.80094	2.07893	2.39656
16	1.37279	1.48451	1.60471	1.87298	2.18287	2.54035
17	1.40024	1.52162	1.65285	1.94790	2.29202	2.69277
18	1.42825	1.55966	1.70243	2.02582	2.40662	2.85434
19	1.45681	1.59865	1.75351	2.10685	2.52695	3.02560
20	1.48595	1.63862	1.80611	2.19112	2.65330	3.20714
21	1.51567	1.67958	1.86029	2.27877	2.78596	3.39956
22	1.54598	1.72157	1.91610	2.36992	2.92526	3.60354
23	1.57690	1.76461	1.97359	2.46472	3.07152	3.81975
24	1.60844	1.80873	2.03279	2.56330	3.22510	4.04893
25	1.64061	1.85394	2.09378	2.66584	3.38635	4.29187
26	1.67342	1.90029	2.15659	2.77247	3.55567	4.54938
27	1.70689	1.94780	2.22129	2.88337	3.73346	4.82235
28	1.74102	1.99650	2.28793	2.99870	3.92013	5.11169
29	1.77584	2.04641	2.35657	3.11865	4.11614	5.41839
30	1.81136	2.09757	2.42726	3.24340	4.32194	5.74349
31	1.84759	2.15001	2.50008	3.37313	4.53804	6.08810
32	1.88454	2.20376	2.57508	3.50806	4.76494	6.45339
33	1.92223	2.25885	2.65234	3.64838	5.00319	6.84059
34	1.96068	2.31532	2.73191	3.79432	5.25335	7.25103
35	1.99989	2.37321	2.81386	3.94609	5.51602	7.68609
36	2.03989	2.43254	2.89828	4.10393	5.79182	8.14725
37	2.08069	2.49335	2.98523	4.26809	6.08141	8.63609
38	2.12230	2.55568	3.07478	4.43881	6.38548	9.15425
39	2.16474	2.61957	3.16703	4.61637	6.70475	9.70351
40	2.20804	2.68506	3.26204	4.80102	7.03999	10.28572

FUTURE AMOUNT OF 1 TABLE 6-1

8%	9%	10%	11%	12%	15%	(n) Periods
1.08000	1.09000	1.10000	1.11000	1.12000	1.15000	1
1.16640	1.18810	1.21000	1.23210	1.25440	1.32250	2
1.25971	1.29503	1.33100	1.36763	1.40493	1.52088	3
1.36049	1.41158	1.46410	1.51807	1.57352	1.74901	4
1.46933	1.53862	1.61051	1.68506	1.76234	2.01136	5
1.58687	1.67710	1.77156	1.87041	1.97382	2.31306	6
1.71382	1.82804	1.94872	2.07616	2.21068	2.66002	7
1.85093	1.99256	2.14359	2.30454	2.47596	3.05902	8
1.99900	2.17189	2.35795	2.55803	2.77308	3.51788	9
2.15892	2.36736	2.59374	2.83942	3.10585	4.04556	10
2.33164	2.58043	2.85312	3.15176	3.47855	4.65239	11
2.51817	2.81267	3.13843	3.49845	3.89598	5.35025	12
2.71962	3.06581	3.45227	3.88328	4.36349	6.15279	13
2.93719	3.34173	3.79750	4.31044	4.88711	7.07571	14
3.17217	3.64248	4.17725	4.78459	5.47357	8.13706	15
3.42594	3.97031	4.59497	5.31089	6.13039	9.35762	16
3.70002	4.32763	5.05447	5.89509	6.86604	10.76126	17
3.99602	4.71712	5.55992	6.54355	7.68997	12.37545	18
4.31570	5.14166	6.11591	7.26334	8.61276	14.23177	19
4.66096	5.60441	6.72750	8.06231	9.64629	16.36654	20
5.03383	6.10881	7.40025	8.94917	10.80385	18.82152	21
5.43654	6.65860	8.14028	9.93357	12.10031	21.64475	22
5.87146	7.25787	8.95430	11.02627	13.55235	24.89146	23
6.34118	7.91108	9.84973	12.23916	15.17863	28.62518	24
6.84847	8.62308	10.83471	13.58546	17.00000	32.91895	25
7.39635	9.39916	11.91818	15.07986	19.04007	37.85680	26
7.98806	10.24508	13.10999	16.73865	21.32488	43.53532	27
8.62711	11.16714	14.42099	18.57990	23.88387	50.06561	28
9.31727	12.17218	15.86309	20.62369	26.74993	57.57545	29
10.06266	13.26768	17.44940	22.89230	29.95992	66.21177	30
10.86767	14.46177	19.19434	25.41045	33.55511	76.14354	31
11.73708	15.76333	21.11378	28.20560	37.58173	87.56507	32
12.67605	17.18203	23.22515	31.30821	42.09153	100.69983	33
13.69013	18.72841	25.54767	34.75212	47.14252	115.80480	34
14.78534	20.41397	28.10244	38.57485	52.79962	133.17552	35
15.96817	22.25123	30.91268	42.81808	59.13557	153.15185	36
17.24563	24.25384	34.00395	47.52807	66.23184	176.12463	37
18.62528	26.43668	37.40434	52.75616	74.17966	202.54332	38
20.11530	28.81598	41.14479	58.55934	83.08122	232.92482	39
21.72452	31.40942	45.25926	65.00087	93.05097	267.86355	40

TABLE 6-2 PRESENT VALUE OF 1 (Present Value of a Single Sum)

$$p_{\overline{n}|i} = \frac{1}{(1+i)^n} = (1+i)^{-n}$$

(n) Periods	2%	2½%	3%	4%	5%	6%
1	.98039	.97561	.97087	.96154	.95238	.94340
2	.96117	.95181	.94260	.92456	.90703	.89000
3	.94232	.92860	.91514	.88900	.86384	.83962
4	.92385	.90595	.88849	.85480	.82270	.79209
5	.90573	.88385	.86261	.82193	.78353	.74726
6	.88797	.86230	.83748	.79031	.74622	.70496
7	.87056	.84127	.81309	.75992	.71068	.66506
8	.85349	.82075	.78941	.73069	.67684	.62741
9	.83676	.80073	.76642	.70259	.64461	.59190
10	.82035	.78120	.74409	.67556	.61391	.55839
11	.80426	.76214	.72242	.64958	.58468	.52679
12	.78849	.74356	.70138	.62460	.55684	.49697
13	.77303	.72542	.68095	.60057	.53032	.46884
14	.75788	.70773	.66112	.57748	.50507	.44230
15	.74301	.69047	.64186	.55526	.48102	.41727
16	.72845	.67362	.62317	.53391	.45811	.39365
17	.71416	.65720	.60502	.51337	.43630	.37136
18	.70016	.64117	.58739	.49363	.41552	.35034
19	.68643	.62553	.57029	.47464	.39573	.33051
20	.67297	.61027	.55368	.45639	.37689	.31180
21	.65978	.59539	.53755	.43883	.35894	.29416
22	.64684	.58086	.52189	.42196	.34185	.27751
23	.63416	.56670	.50669	.40573	.32557	.26180
24	.62172	.55288	.49193	.39012	.31007	.24698
25	.60953	.53939	.47761	.37512	.29530	.23300
26	.59758	.52623	.46369	.36069	.28124	.21981
27	.58586	.51340	.45019	.34682	.26785	.20737
28	.57437	.50088	.43708	.33348	.25509	.19563
29	.56311	.48866	.42435	.32065	.24295	.18456
30	.55207	.47674	.41199	.30832	.23138	.17411
31	.54125	.46511	.39999	.29646	.22036	.16425
32	.53063	.45377	.38834	.28506	.20987	.15496
33	.52023	.44270	.37703	.27409	.19987	.14619
34	.51003	.43191	.36604	.26355	.19035	.13791
35	.50003	.42137	.35538	.25342	.18129	.13011
36	.49022	.41109	.34503	.24367	.17266	.12274
37	.48061	.40107	.33498	.23430	.16444	.11579
38	.47119	.39128	.32523	.22529	.15661	.10924
39	.46195	.38174	.31575	.21662	.14915	.10306
40	.45289	.37243	.30656	.20829	.14205	.09722

PRESENT VALUE OF 1 TABLE 6-2

8%	9%	10%	11%	12%	15%	(n) Periods
.92593	.91743	.90909	.90090	.89286	.86957	1
.85734	.84168	.82645	.81162	.79719	.75614	2
.79383	.77218	.75132	.73119	.71178	.65752	3
.73503	.70843	.68301	.65873	.63552	.57175	4
.68058	.64993	.62092	.59345	.56743	.49718	5
.63017	.59627	.56447	.53464	.50663	.43233	6
.58349	.54703	.51316	.48166	.45235	.37594	7
.54027	.50187	.46651	.43393	.40388	.32690	8
.50025	.46043	.42410	.39092	.36061	.28426	9
.46319	.42241	.38554	.35218	.32197	.24719	10
.42888	.38753	.35049	.31728	.28748	.21494	11
.39711	.35554	.31863	.28584	.25668	.18691	12
.36770	.32618	.28966	.25751	.22917	.16253	13
.34046	.29925	.26333	.23199	.20462	.14133	14
.31524	.27454	.23939	.20900	.18270	.12289	15
.29189	.25187	.21763	.18829	.16312	.10687	16
.27027	.23107	.19785	.16963	.14564	.09293	17
.25025	.21199	.17986	.15282	.13004	.08081	18
.23171	.19449	.16351	.13768	.11611	.07027	19
.21455	.17843	.14864	.12403	.10367	.06110	20
.19866	.16370	.13513	.11174	.09256	.05313	21
.18394	.15018	.12285	.10067	.08264	.04620	22
.17032	.13778	.11168	.09069	.07379	.04017	23
.15770	.12641	.10153	.08170	.06588	.03493	24
.14602	.11597	.09230	.07361	.05882	.03038	25
.13520	.10639	.08391	.06631	.05252	.02642	26
.12519	.09761	.07628	.05974	.04689	.02297	27
.11591	.08955	.06934	.05382	.04187	.01997	28
.10733	.08216	.06304	.04849	.03738	.01737	29
.09938	.07537	.05731	.04368	.03338	.01510	30
.09202	.06915	.05210	.03935	.02980	.01313	31
.08520	.06344	.04736	.03545	.02661	.01142	32
.07889	.05820	.04306	.03194	.02376	.00993	33
.07305	.05340	.03914	.02878	.02121	.00864	34
.06763	.04899	.03558	.02592	.01894	.00751	35
.06262	.04494	.03235	.02335	.01691	.00653	36
.05799	.04123	.02941	.02104	.01510	.00568	37
.05369	.03783	.02674	.01896	.01348	.00494	38
.04971	.03470	.02430	.01708	.01204	.00429	39
.04603	.03184	.02210	.01538	.01075	.00373	40

TABLE 6–3 FUTURE AMOUNT OF AN ORDINARY ANNUITY OF 1

$$A_{\overline{n}|i} = \frac{(1+i)^n - 1}{i}$$

(n) Periods	2%	2½%	3%	4%	5%	6%
1	1.00000	1.00000	1.00000	1.00000	1.00000	1.00000
2	2.02000	2.02500	2.03000	2.04000	2.05000	2.06000
3	3.06040	3.07563	3.09090	3.12160	3.15250	3.18360
4	4.12161	4.15252	4.18363	4.24646	4.31013	4.37462
5	5.20404	5.25633	5.30914	5.41632	5.52563	5.63709
6	6.30812	6.38774	6.46841	6.63298	6.80191	6.97532
7	7.43428	7.54743	7.66246	7.89829	8.14201	8.39384
8	8.58297	8.73612	8.89234	9.21423	9.54911	9.89747
9	9.75463	9.95452	10.15911	10.58280	11.02656	11.49132
10	10.94972	11.20338	11.46338	12.00611	12.57789	13.18079
11	12.16872	12.48347	12.80780	13.48635	14.20679	14.97164
12	13.41209	13.79555	14.19203	15.02581	15.91713	16.86994
13	14.68033	15.14044	15.61779	16.62684	17.71298	18.88214
14	15.97394	16.51895	17.08632	18.29191	19.59863	21.01507
15	17.29342	17.93193	18.59891	20.02359	21.57856	23.27597
16	18.63929	19.38022	20.15688	21.82453	23.65749	25.67253
17	20.01207	20.86473	21.76159	23.69751	25.84037	28.21288
18	21.41231	22.38635	23.41444	25.64541	28.13238	30.90565
19	22.84056	23.94601	25.11687	27.67123	30.53900	33.75999
20	24.29737	25.54466	26.87037	29.77808	33.06595	36.78559
21	25.78332	27.18327	28.67649	31.96920	35.71925	39.99273
22	27.29898	28.86286	30.53678	34.24797	38.50521	43.39229
23	28.84496	30.58443	32.45288	36.61789	41.43048	46.99583
24	30.42186	32.34904	34.42647	39.08260	44.50200	50.81558
25	32.03030	34.15776	36.45926	41.64591	47.72710	54.86451
26	33.67091	36.01171	38.55304	44.31174	51.11345	59.15638
27	35.34432	37.91200	40.70963	47.08421	54.66913	63.70577
28	37.05121	39.85980	42.93092	49.96758	58.40258	68.52811
29	38.79223	41.85630	45.21885	52.96629	62.32271	73.63980
30	40.56808	43.90270	47.57542	56.08494	66.43885	79.05819
31	42.37944	46.00027	50.00268	59.32834	70.76079	84.80168
32	44.22703	48.15028	52.50276	62.70147	75.29883	90.88978
33	46.11157	50.35403	55.07784	66.20953	80.06377	97.34316
34	48.03380	52.61289	57.73018	69.85791	85.06696	104.18376
35	49.99448	54.92821	60.46208	73.65222	90.32031	111.43478
36	51.99437	57.30141	63.27594	77.59831	95.83632	119.12087
37	54.03425	59.73395	66.17422	81.70225	101.62814	127.26812
38	56.11494	62.22730	69.15945	85.97034	107.70955	135.90421
39	58.23724	64.78298	72.23423	90.40915	114.09502	145.05846
40	60.40198	67.40255	75.40126	95.02552	120.79977	154.76197

FUTURE AMOUNT OF AN ORDINARY ANNUITY OF 1   TABLE 6-3

8%	9%	10%	11%	12%	15%	(n) Periods
1.00000	1.00000	1.00000	1.00000	1.00000	1.00000	1
2.08000	2.09000	2.10000	2.11000	2.12000	2.15000	2
3.24640	3.27810	3.31000	3.34210	3.37440	3.47250	3
4.50611	4.57313	4.64100	4.70973	4.77933	4.99338	4
5.86660	5.98471	6.10510	6.22780	6.35285	6.74238	5
7.33592	7.52334	7.71561	7.91286	8.11519	8.75374	6
8.92280	9.20044	9.48717	9.78327	10.08901	11.06680	7
10.63663	11.02847	11.43589	11.85943	12.29969	13.72682	8
12.48756	13.02104	13.57948	14.16397	14.77566	16.78584	9
14.48656	15.19293	15.93743	16.72201	17.54874	20.30372	10
16.64549	17.56029	18.53117	19.56143	20.65458	24.34928	11
18.97713	20.14072	21.38428	22.71319	24.13313	29.00167	12
21.49530	22.95339	24.52271	26.21164	28.02911	34.35192	13
24.21492	26.01919	27.97498	30.09492	32.39260	40.50471	14
27.15211	29.36092	31.77248	34.40536	37.27972	47.58041	15
30.32428	33.00340	35.94973	39.18995	42.75328	55.71747	16
33.75023	36.97371	40.54470	44.50084	48.88367	65.07509	17
37.45024	41.30134	45.59917	50.39593	55.74972	75.83636	18
41.44626	46.01846	51.15909	56.93949	63.43968	88.21181	19
45.76196	51.16012	57.27500	64.20283	72.05244	102.44358	20
50.42292	56.76453	64.00250	72.26514	81.69874	118.81012	21
55.45676	62.87334	71.40275	81.21431	92.50258	137.63164	22
60.89330	69.53194	79.54302	91.14788	104.60289	159.27638	23
66.76476	76.78981	88.49733	102.17415	118.15524	184.16784	24
73.10594	84.70090	98.34706	114.41331	133.33387	212.79302	25
79.95442	93.32398	109.18177	127.99877	150.33393	245.71197	26
87.35077	102.72314	121.09994	143.07864	169.37401	283.56877	27
95.33883	112.96822	134.20994	159.81729	190.69889	327.10408	28
103.96594	124.13536	148.63093	178.39719	214.58275	377.16969	29
113.28321	136.30754	164.49402	199.02088	241.33268	434.74515	30
123.34587	149.57522	181.94343	221.91317	271.29261	500.95692	31
134.21354	164.03699	201.13777	247.32362	304.84772	577.10046	32
145.95062	179.80032	222.25154	275.52922	342.42945	644.66553	33
158.62667	196.98234	245.47670	306.83744	384.52098	765.36535	34
172.31680	215.71076	271.02437	341.58955	431.66350	881.17016	35
187.10215	236.12472	299.12681	380.16441	484.46312	1014.34568	36
203.07032	258.37595	330.03949	422.98249	543.59869	1167.49753	37
220.31595	282.62978	364.04343	470.51056	609.83053	1343.62216	38
238.94122	309.06646	401.44778	523.26673	684.01020	1546.16549	39
259.05652	337.88245	442.59256	581.82607	767.09142	1779.09031	40

TABLE 6-4 PRESENT VALUE OF AN ORDINARY ANNUITY OF 1

$$P_{\overline{n}|i} = \frac{1 - \frac{1}{(1+i)^n}}{i} = \frac{1 - p_{\overline{n}|i}}{i}$$

(n) Periods	2%	2½%	3%	4%	5%	6%
1	.98039	.97561	.97087	.96154	.95238	.94340
2	1.94156	1.92742	1.91347	1.88609	1.85941	1.83339
3	2.88388	2.85602	2.82861	2.77509	2.72325	2.67301
4	3.80773	3.76197	3.71710	3.62990	3.54595	3.46511
5	4.71346	4.64583	4.57971	4.45182	4.32948	4.21236
6	5.60143	5.50813	5.41719	5.24214	5.07569	4.91732
7	6.47199	6.34939	6.23028	6.00205	5.78637	5.58238
8	7.32548	7.17014	7.01969	6.73274	6.46321	6.20979
9	8.16224	7.97087	7.78611	7.43533	7.10782	6.80169
10	8.98259	8.75206	8.53020	8.11090	7.72173	7.36009
11	9.78685	9.51421	9.25262	8.76048	8.30641	7.88687
12	10.57534	10.25776	9.95400	9.38507	8.86325	8.38384
13	11.34837	10.98319	10.63496	9.98565	9.39357	8.85268
14	12.10625	11.69091	11.29607	10.56312	9.89864	9.29498
15	12.84926	12.38138	11.93794	11.11839	10.37966	9.71225
16	13.57771	13.05500	12.56110	11.65230	10.83777	10.10590
17	14.29187	13.71220	13.16612	12.16567	11.27407	10.47726
18	14.99203	14.35336	13.75351	12.65930	11.68959	10.82760
19	15.67846	14.97889	14.32380	13.13394	12.08532	11.15812
20	16.35143	15.58916	14.87747	13.59033	12.46221	11.46992
21	17.01121	16.18455	15.41502	14.02916	12.82115	11.76408
22	17.65805	16.76541	15.93692	14.45112	13.16300	12.04158
23	18.29220	17.33211	16.44361	14.85684	13.48857	12.30338
24	18.91393	17.88499	16.93554	15.24696	13.79864	12.55036
25	19.52346	18.42438	17.41315	15.62208	14.09394	12.78336
26	20.12104	18.95061	17.87684	15.98277	14.37519	13.00317
27	20.70690	19.46401	18.32703	16.32959	14.64303	13.21053
28	21.28127	19.96489	18.76411	16.66306	14.89813	13.40616
29	21.84438	20.45355	19.18845	16.98371	15.14107	13.59072
30	22.39646	20.93029	19.60044	17.29203	15.37245	13.76483
31	22.93770	21.39541	20.00043	17.58849	15.59281	13.92909
32	23.46833	21.84918	20.38877	17.87355	15.80268	14.08404
33	23.98856	22.29188	20.76579	18.14765	16.00255	14.23023
34	24.49859	22.72379	21.13184	18.41120	16.19290	14.36814
35	24.99862	23.14516	21.48722	18.66461	16.37419	14.49825
36	25.48884	23.55625	21.83225	18.90828	16.54685	14.62099
37	25.96945	23.95732	22.16724	19.14258	16.71129	14.73678
38	26.44064	24.34860	22.49246	19.36786	16.86789	14.84602
39	26.90259	24.73034	22.80822	19.58448	17.01704	14.94907
40	27.35548	25.10278	23.11477	19.79277	17.15909	15.04630

PRESENT VALUE OF AN ORDINARY ANNUITY OF 1   TABLE 6-4

8%	9%	10%	11%	12%	15%	(n) Periods
.92593	.91743	.90909	.90090	.89286	.86957	1
1.78326	1.75911	1.73554	1.71252	1.69005	1.62571	2
2.57710	2.53130	2.48685	2.44371	2.40183	2.28323	3
3.31213	3.23972	3.16986	3.10245	3.03735	2.85498	4
3.99271	3.88965	3.79079	3.69590	3.60478	3.35216	5
4.62288	4.48592	4.35526	4.23054	4.11141	3.78448	6
5.20637	5.03295	4.86842	4.71220	4.56376	4.16042	7
5.74664	5.53482	5.33493	5.14612	4.96764	4.48732	8
6.24689	5.99525	5.75902	5.53705	5.32825	4.77158	9
6.71008	6.41766	6.14457	5.88923	5.65022	5.01877	10
7.13896	6.80519	6.49506	6.20652	5.93770	5.23371	11
7.53608	7.16073	6.81369	6.49236	6.19437	5.42062	12
7.90378	7.48690	7.10336	6.74987	6.42355	5.58315	13
8.24424	7.78615	7.36669	6.98187	6.62817	5.72448	14
8.55948	8.06069	7.60608	7.19087	6.81086	5.84737	15
8.85137	8.31256	7.82371	7.37916	6.97399	5.95424	16
9.12164	8.54363	8.02155	7.54879	7.11963	6.04716	17
9.37189	8.75563	8.20141	7.70162	7.24967	6.12797	18
9.60360	8.95012	8.36492	7.83929	7.36578	6.19823	19
9.81815	9.12855	8.51356	7.96333	7.46944	6.25933	20
10.01680	9.29224	8.64869	8.07507	7.56200	6.31246	21
10.20074	9.44243	8.77154	8.17574	7.64465	6.35866	22
10.37106	9.58021	8.88322	8.26643	7.71843	6.39884	23
10.52876	9.70661	8.98474	8.34814	7.78432	6.43377	24
10.67478	9.82258	9.07704	8.42174	7.84314	6.46415	25
10.80998	9.92897	9.16095	8.48806	7.89566	6.49056	26
10.93516	10.02658	9.23722	8.54780	7.94255	6.51353	27
11.05108	10.11613	9.30657	8.60162	7.98442	6.53351	28
11.15841	10.19828	9.36961	8.65011	8.02181	6.55088	29
11.25778	10.27365	9.42691	8.69379	8.05518	6.56598	30
11.34980	10.34280	9.47901	8.73315	8.08499	6.57911	31
11.43500	10.40624	9.52638	8.76860	8.11159	6.59053	32
11.51389	10.46444	9.56943	8.80054	8.13535	6.60046	33
11.58693	10.51784	9.60858	8.82932	8.15656	6.60910	34
11.65457	10.56682	9.64416	8.85524	8.17550	6.61661	35
11.71719	10.61176	9.67651	8.87859	8.19241	6.62314	36
11.77518	10.65299	9.70592	8.89963	8.20751	6.62882	37
11.82887	10.69082	9.73265	8.91859	8.22099	6.63375	38
11.87858	10.72552	9.75697	8.93567	8.23303	6.63805	39
11.92461	10.75736	9.77905	8.95105	8.24378	6.64178	40

TABLE 6-5 PRESENT VALUE OF AN ANNUITY DUE OF 1

$$Pd_{\overline{n}|i} = 1 + \frac{1 - \frac{1}{(1+i)^{n-1}}}{i} = (1+i)\left(\frac{1 - P_{\overline{n}|i}}{i}\right) = (1+i) P_{\overline{n}|i}$$

(n) Periods	2%	2½%	3%	4%	5%	6%
1	1.00000	1.00000	1.00000	1.00000	1.00000	1.00000
2	1.98039	1.97561	1.97087	1.96154	1.95238	1.94340
3	2.94156	2.92742	2.91347	2.88609	2.85941	2.83339
4	3.88388	3.85602	3.82861	3.77509	3.72325	3.67301
5	4.80773	4.76197	4.71710	4.62990	4.54595	4.46511
6	5.71346	5.64583	5.57971	5.45182	5.32948	5.21236
7	6.60143	6.50813	6.41719	6.24214	6.07569	5.91732
8	7.47199	7.34939	7.23028	7.00205	6.78637	6.58238
9	8.32548	8.17014	8.01969	7.73274	7.46321	7.20979
10	9.16224	8.97087	8.78611	8.43533	8.10782	7.80169
11	9.98259	9.75206	9.53020	9.11090	8.72173	8.36009
12	10.78685	10.51421	10.25262	9.76048	9.30641	8.88687
13	11.57534	11.25776	10.95400	10.38507	9.86325	9.38384
14	12.34837	11.98319	11.63496	10.98565	10.39357	9.85268
15	13.10625	12.69091	12.29607	11.56312	10.89864	10.29498
16	13.84926	13.38138	12.93794	12.11839	11.37966	10.71225
17	14.57771	14.05500	13.56110	12.65230	11.83777	11.10590
18	15.29187	14.71220	14.16612	13.16567	12.27407	11.47726
19	15.99203	15.35336	14.75351	13.65930	12.68959	11.82760
20	16.67846	15.97889	15.32380	14.13394	13.08532	12.15812
21	17.35143	16.58916	15.87747	14.59033	13.46221	12.46992
22	18.01121	17.18455	16.41502	15.02916	13.82115	12.76408
23	18.65805	17.76541	16.93692	15.45112	14.16300	13.04158
24	19.29220	18.33211	17.44361	15.85684	14.48857	13.30338
25	19.91393	18.88499	17.93554	16.24696	14.79864	13.55036
26	20.52346	19.42438	18.41315	16.62208	15.09394	13.78336
27	21.12104	19.95061	18.87684	16.98277	15.37519	14.00317
28	21.70690	20.46401	19.32703	17.32959	15.64303	14.21053
29	22.28127	20.96489	19.76411	17.66306	15.89813	14.40616
30	22.84438	21.45355	20.18845	17.98371	16.14107	14.59072
31	23.39646	21.93029	20.60044	18.29203	16.37245	14.76483
32	23.93770	22.39541	21.00043	18.58849	16.59281	14.92909
33	24.46833	22.84918	21.38877	18.87355	16.80268	15.08404
34	24.98856	23.29188	21.76579	19.14765	17.00255	15.23023
35	25.49859	23.72379	22.13184	19.41120	17.19290	15.36814
36	25.99862	24.14516	22.48722	19.66461	17.37419	15.49825
37	26.48884	24.55625	22.83225	19.90828	17.54685	15.62099
38	26.96945	24.95732	23.16724	20.14258	17.71129	15.73678
39	27.44064	25.34860	23.49246	20.36786	17.86789	15.84602
40	27.90259	25.73034	23.80822	20.58448	18.01704	15.94907

PRESENT VALUE OF AN ANNUITY DUE OF 1   TABLE 6-5

8%	9%	10%	11%	12%	15%	(n) Periods
1.00000	1.00000	1.00000	1.00000	1.00000	1.00000	1
1.92593	1.91743	1.90909	1.90090	1.89286	1.86957	2
2.78326	2.75911	2.73554	2.71252	2.69005	2.62571	3
3.57710	3.53130	3.48685	3.44371	3.40183	3.28323	4
4.31213	4.23972	4.16986	4.10245	4.03735	3.85498	5
4.99271	4.88965	4.79079	4.69590	4.60478	4.35216	6
5.62288	5.48592	5.35526	5.23054	5.11141	4.78448	7
6.20637	6.03295	5.86842	5.71220	5.56376	5.16042	8
6.74664	6.53482	6.33493	6.14612	5.96764	5.48732	9
7.24689	6.99525	6.75902	6.53705	6.32825	5.77158	10
7.71008	7.41766	7.14457	6.88923	6.65022	6.01877	11
8.13896	7.80519	7.49506	7.20652	6.93770	6.23371	12
8.53608	8.16073	7.81369	7.49236	7.19437	6.42062	13
8.90378	8.48690	8.10336	7.74987	7.42355	6.58315	14
9.24424	8.78615	8.36669	7.98187	7.62817	6.72448	15
9.55948	9.06069	8.60608	8.19087	7.81086	6.84737	16
9.85137	9.31256	8.82371	8.37916	7.97399	6.95424	17
10.12164	9.54363	9.02155	8.54879	8.11963	7.04716	18
10.37189	9.75563	9.20141	8.70162	8.24967	7.12797	19
10.60360	9.95012	9.36492	8.83929	8.36578	7.19823	20
10.81815	10.12855	9.51356	8.96333	8.46944	7.25933	21
11.01680	10.29224	9.64869	9.07507	8.56200	7.31246	22
11.20074	10.44243	9.77154	9.17574	8.64465	7.35866	23
11.37106	10.58021	9.88322	9.26643	8.71843	7.39884	24
11.52876	10.70661	9.98474	9.34814	8.78432	7.43377	25
11.67478	10.82258	10.07704	9.42174	8.84314	7.46415	26
11.80998	10.92897	10.16095	9.48806	8.89566	7.49056	27
11.93518	11.02658	10.23722	9.54780	8.94255	7.51353	28
12.05108	11.11613	10.30657	9.60162	8.98442	7.53351	29
12.15841	11.19828	10.36961	9.65011	9.02181	7.55088	30
12.25778	11.27365	10.42691	9.69379	9.05518	7.56598	31
12.34980	11.34280	10.47901	9.73315	9.08499	7.57911	32
12.43500	11.40624	10.52638	9.76860	9.11159	7.59053	33
12.51389	11.46444	10.56943	9.80054	9.13535	7.60046	34
12.58693	11.51784	10.60858	9.82932	9.15656	7.60910	35
12.65457	11.56682	10.64416	9.85524	9.17550	7.61661	36
12.71719	11.61176	10.67651	9.87859	9.19241	7.62314	37
12.77518	11.65299	10.70592	9.89963	9.20751	7.62882	38
12.82887	11.69082	10.73265	9.91859	9.22099	7.63375	39
12.87858	11.72552	10.75697	9.93567	9.23303	7.63805	40

GLOSSARY

ABSORPTION COSTING: a method of product costing that assigns fixed manufacturing overhead to the units produced.

ACTUAL COSTING: the allocation of costs to products according to actual direct materials consumed, direct labour used, and overhead incurred.

ADMINISTRATIVE EXPENSES: expenses incurred by the managerial and policy-making aspects of a business.

ALLOCATION: assignment of items of cost or revenue to one or more segments of an organization according to benefits received or some other logical measure of use.

BREAK-EVEN MODEL: a model showing the relationships among units produced (output), dollars of sales revenue, and the levels of costs and profits for a firm or a product line.

BREAK-EVEN POINT: the level of activity (volume) at which a company earns zero profits, occurring when total revenue equals total expenses.

CA: Chartered Accountant (Canada).

CANADIAN INSTITUTE OF CHARTERED ACCOUNTANTS (CICA): the association of provincial institutes (ordre in Quebec) which confers the CA designation and safeguards professional standards and ethics in Canada.

CAPITAL BUDGET: a budget that identifies expenditures for buildings and capital goods and which identifies the sources of the funds required to meet the expenditures.

CAPITAL BUDGETING: the process of identifying and evaluating capital investment projects for a capital expenditure budget.

CAPITAL COST ALLOWANCE: sums set aside in financial statements to write off the initial costs of investments or equipment, buildings, and improvements to land, usually treated as a cost of production; synonymous with depreciation.

CASH BUDGET: a schedule of cash receipts and disbursements.

CASH FLOW: the net income of a corporation plus amounts charged off for depreciation, depletion, amortization, and extraordinary charges, which are not actually paid out in cash.

COMMITTED FIXED COSTS: costs that do not vary over a relevant range of activity and that cannot be readily changed.

COMMON COST: a cost that is common to all the segments of a business and cannot practically be allocated among them.

CONTRIBUTION MARGIN: the excess of revenue over variable cost.

CONTROL: the concept of monitoring activities and taking action to correct undesirable performance.

CONTROL ACCOUNT: a summary account in the general ledger that is supported by detailed individual accounts.

CONTROLLABLE MARKETING ACTIVITIES: those marketing activities over which a firm has control, such as the product, its name, its packaging, its advertising, its pricing, its sales promotion, and the method of distribution.

CONVERSION COSTS: the combination of direct labour and factor overhead costs in manufacturing.

COST: the value given up in order to receive goods or services; all expenses are costs, but not all costs are expenses.

COST ACCOUNTING: a branch of accounting that deals with the classification, recording, allocation, and reporting of current and prospective costs.

COST AFTER SPLIT-OFF: the production cost of joint products that occurs after the split-off point and is identifiable with a specific product.

COST ALLOCATION: the assignment of common costs to cost centres in accordance with the matching principle.

COST BEHAVIOUR: the changes in a cost with respect to changes in the level of activity, usually classified as fixed, variable, semi-fixed, semi-variable, or mixed.

COST-BENEFIT ANALYSIS: a branch of operations research that aids in evaluating alternative courses of action; it is primarily concerned with the selection of equipment, products, etc.

COST CENTRE: a responsibility centre in management accounting which is held accountable for the costs under its control.

COST OF CAPITAL: the weighted-average cost of a firm's debt and equity capital; also the rate of return that a company must earn to satisfy the demands of owners and creditors.

COST OF GOODS MANUFACTURED: all direct material costs, labour costs, and overhead costs transferred from work in process inventory to finished goods inventory.

COST OF GOODS SOLD: the costs incurred for goods sold during a specified period, including transportation costs.

COST PLUS PRICING: the practice of adding a percentage or amount to the cost of goods to establish the selling price.

COST POOL: a set of costs allocated to cost centres in some plausible way.

COST-VOLUME PROFIT ANALYSIS: a method used for examining the functional relationships among the major aspects of profits and for identifying the profit structure.

CPA: Certified Public Accountant (United States).

CPP: abbreviation for Canada Pension Plan.

DATA BASE: a collection of information specific to an organization.

DECENTRALIZATION: the placing of the decision-making point at the lowest managerial level, involving delegation of decision-making authority.

DECISION MAKER: a person who has the authority to make a decision either alone or as part of a group.

DEMAND: the desire and ability to purchase goods or services.

DEMAND CURVE: a graphic representation of the quantity of goods demanded in relation to their price.

DIFFERENTIAL COSTS: the difference in costs between two situations.

DIRECT ALLOCATION: the allocation of service department overhead costs directly to producing departments without allocation to other service departments.

DIRECT COST: the cost of a good or service that contributes to the production of a commodity or service.

DIRECT COSTING: a technique for implementing marginal analysis to assist in making short-term business decisions.

DIRECT LABOUR: the dollar value of wages paid to workers.

DIRECT MATERIAL: raw material that is part of the finished good and can be assigned to specific physical units.

DISCOUNTED CASH FLOW METHODS: capital budgeting techniques that take into account the time value of money.

DISCOUNTED RATE OF RETURN: the rate of return that equates future cash inflows with cash outflows of an investment.

DISCRETIONARY COSTS: fixed costs arising from periodic, decisions that directly reflect top-management policies and can be varied by its actions.

DIVISIONALIZATION: the existence of autonomous units in an organization; responsibility for performance rests with a divisional or sectional manager who operates the division as if it were separate from the parent organization.

EFFICIENCY VARIANCE: quantity variance for labour.

EOQ (economic order quantity) MODEL: an inventory decision-making approach used to create a formula for determining what quantity of supplies to order.

FACTORY OVERHEAD: manufacturing costs that are not direct material and direct labour.

FACTORY OVERHEAD INCURRED: manufacturing costs (not including direct material and direct labour) incurred during a given accounting period.

FAVOURABLE VARIANCE: the amount by which standard costs exceed actual costs.

FIFO (first in-first out): a term relating to inventory valuations that means that the cost shown for the first shipment of an item is used for valuation in accounting.

FINANCIAL ACCOUNTING: the area of accounting concerned with measuring and reporting on the financial status and operating results of an organization.

FINANCIAL ANALYSIS: the use of specific techniques to study a firm's financial statements.

FINANCIAL CONTROLS: the vital factors in control processes; namely budgets, financial analysis, and break-even analysis.

FINANCIAL EXPENSE: interest expense on long-term debt.

FINANCIAL POSITION: the financial status of a company, indicated by the assets and liabilities on a balance sheet.

FINANCIAL REPORTING: periodic reporting of the financial position of an organization in terms of operating results and financial transactions.

FINISHED-GOODS INVENTORY: all completed, manufactured items made for sale to customers.

FIXED ASSETS: permanent assets required for the normal conduct of a business which normally are not converted into cash (e.g. fixtures, buildings and land).

FIXED BUDGET: a budget that remains the same after it is established, regardless of the activity level of the organization or program.

FIXED CHARGES: business expenses not related to the level of activity.

FIXED COST (expense): a cost (expense) for a fixed period and range of activity that does not change in total.

FIXED OVERHEAD: the portion of manufacturing overhead that does not change with the level of activity.

FLEXIBLE BUDGET: a budget that is established for a range rather than for a single level of activity.

FULL-COST PRICING: the practice of including all appropriate manufacturing costs in determining inventory values and prices.

FUND (working capital): current assets less current liabilities.

GROSS MARGIN: amount determined by subtracting cost of goods sold from net sales. (Synonymous with gross profit.)

GROSS REVENUE: revenues received from selling goods or performing services before any deductions have been made for returns, allowances, or discounts.

HISTORICAL COST: the principle requiring that all financial statements be presented in terms of the item's original cost to the entity.

IDLE TIME: time when an employee is not working because of machine malfunction or other factors not within the control of the worker.

INDIRECT COSTS: costs not identifiable with or incurred as the result of the manufacture of specific goods or services but applicable to a productive activity generally.

INDIRECT LABOUR COSTS: cost of wages for non-production employees, such as maintenance crews, inspectors, timekeepers, tool crib attendants, and sweepers.

INDIRECT MATERIAL COSTS: the costs of materials that are included as manufacturing overhead and assigned to products on a reasonable basis.

INVENTORY CONTROL: the control of goods on hand by accounting and physical methods.

INVENTORY TURNOVER: the average number of times that inventory is replaced during a period, calculated by dividing cost of goods sold by average inventory.

INVESTMENT CENTRE: a unit of an organization in which a manager has responsibility for costs, revenues, and investments.

JOB-ORDER COSTING: a method of product costing in which each job, product, or batch of products is costed separately.

JOINT COST: a cost that is common to all segments or products in question and that can be assigned only by arbitrary allocation.

JOINT PRODUCTION COSTS: the costs of two or more produced goods made by a single process not identifiable as individual products up to a certain stage of production known as the split-off point.

LABOUR EFFICIENCY VARIANCE: a variance caused by incurring more or fewer labour hours than standard.

LEAD TIME: the elapsed time between the beginning of a function and its completion.

LEARNING CURVE: a graphic representation of the measured changes in costs as the number of units increases.

MAKE-OR-BUY DECISION: a firm's decision about whether to produce an item or purchase it elsewhere.

MANAGEMENT ACCOUNTING: a resource for management that supplies financial information to be used in planning and administering the business.

MANAGEMENT INFORMATION SYSTEM (MIS): a specific system that is designed to furnish management and supervisory personnel with current information in real time; data are recorded and processed for operational purposes; problems are isolated for referral to upper management for decision making.

MANAGERIAL ACCOUNTING: the area of accounting concerned with assisting managers in decision making for planning, budgeting, and controlling costs and revenues.

MANAGERIAL CONTROL: the monitoring and modification of activity and resource use so that predetermined standards are met and plans are carried out.

MANAGERIAL PERFORMANCE: the extent to which a manager achieves coordinated work and results through the efforts of subordinates.

MANUFACTURING COSTS: costs incurred in the process of bringing a product to completion, including direct-materials, direct-labour, and manufacturing overhead costs.

MANUFACTURING INVENTORY: a term covering all items of inventory for a manufacturing entity, including raw materials, work in process, and finished goods.

MANUFACTURING OVERHEAD: all expenses arising from manufacturing activities except labour and materials.

MARGIN: the difference between the cost of items sold and the net sales income.

MARGINAL ANALYSIS: analysis of information by examining the value added in one variable when another variable is increased by a single unit.

MARGINAL COST: the increase in the cost of production that results from manufacturing one more unit.

MARGINAL COST PRICING: the rule in competitive markets that price should equal the cost of producing the final (marginal) unit.

MARGINAL REVENUE: the added revenue received from the sale of one additional unit.

MARGIN OF SAFETY: the amount by which sales exceed the break-even point, providing a cushion against a drop in sales or other unforeseeable forces.

MASTER BUDGET: a budget composed of all the various departmental budgets.

MATERIALS BUDGET: a forecast of the amount of material that will be necessary to achieve a result.

MATERIAL COST: the cost of an item directly resulting from the cost of raw material.

MATERIALITY: the concept that accounting should disclose only those events important enough to have an influence on the reader.

MBO (management by objectives): a process in which superiors and those who report to them jointly establish objectives over a specified time period, meeting periodically to evaluate progress in meeting these goals.

MATERIAL PRICE VARIANCE: a variance incurred by paying more or less than the standard price for a raw material.

MATERIAL QUANTITY VARIANCE: a variance incurred by using more or less material than the standard quantity.

MIXED COSTS: costs including both fixed and variable elements within a relevant range of activity.

MOVING AVERAGE: a perpetual inventory cost-flow assumption in which the cost of goods sold and the ending inventory are determined as a weighted-average cost of all merchandise on hand after each purchase.

NEGOTIATED PRICE: the result obtained by a purchaser who desires something different from what is usually available or who is powerful enough to obtain prices lower than those usually charged.

NET PRESENT VALUE (NPV): the difference between the present values of an investment's expected cash inflows and cash outflows.

NON-MANUFACTURING EXPENSES: expenditures that are not associated with the manufacture of products, but which include selling and administrative expenses.

NORMAL CAPACITY: the expected activity level (however defined) for the accounting period assuming normal operations.

NOT-FOR-PROFIT: describes the activities of an organization established with the goal of providing service for a group in society rather than for the purpose of making a profit.

OPERATING BUDGET: a quantitative expression of a plan of action that shows how a firm will acquire and use its financial resources over a specified period of time.

OPERATING INCOME: income to a business produced by its tangible assets and by fees for services rendered.

OPPORTUNITY COST: the maximum alternative profit that could have been obtained if the productive good, service, or capacity had been applied to the next best use.

ORDERING COST: a major cost component that is considered in inventory control decisions consisting of some clerical and administrative work and labour used in placing the order and putting the items in inventory.

OVER-APPLIED OVERHEAD: the excess of the amount of overhead cost applied to a product over the amount of overhead cost budgeted.

PAYBACK PERIOD: the period of time that passes before the incoming cash flows equal the outgoing cash flows on a specific project.

PERFORMANCE APPRAISAL: a methodical review of performance on the job to evaluate the effectiveness or adequacy of the work.

PHYSICAL UNITS ALLOCATION METHOD: a method of cost allocation in which each unit of product in the product group receives the same amount of joint cost.

PLANNING: an activity that requires establishment of a predetermined course of action, beginning with a statement of goals and objectives.

PRESENT VALUE: the discounted value of a certain sum that is payable for a specified future date.

PRICE: the amount of money received for goods or services at the factory or place of business.

PROCESS COSTING: a method of product costing whereby costs are accumulated by process or work centres and averaged over all products manufactured in the centres for a specified period.

PRODUCT COSTING: the assignment of manufacturing costs to products to determine the cost of finished goods.

PRODUCTION MIX VARIANCE: a measure of the dollar amount of variance caused by a change from the standard mix of production inputs to something else.

PROFIT CENTRE: a segment of a business responsible for both revenues and expenses.

PROFIT MARGIN (per unit): sales less all operating expenses divided by the number of units sold.

PURCHASE PRICE: the dollar amount for which any item can be bought.

RATE VARIANCE: the difference between actual wages paid and the standard wage rate multiplied by the total actual hours of direct labour used.

RAW MATERIAL: unprocessed resources utilized in manufacturing an item.

RELEVANCE: that characteristic of accounting information such that it meets the needs of users.

RELEVANT COST: a cost needed in the decision-making process with two characteristics: it is an expected future cost and it is a differential cost.

REORDER POINT: the inventory level at which an order is placed for some specific item.

RELEVANT RANGE: the band of activity over which budgeted sales and expense; will be valid.

RESIDUAL INCOME: the net income of a profit centre or investment centre less the imputed interest on its assets used.

RESPONSIBILITY ACCOUNTING: a system under which a manager is held responsible for each activity that occurs in his particular area of the firm.

RESPONSIBILITY CENTRE: an unit in an organization for which the manager has control over and is held accountable for either costs, costs and revenues, or costs, revenues, and investments.

ROI (return on investment): the dollar amount earned divided by the capital invested.

SAFETY STOCK: a minimum inventory providing a cushion against reasonably expected maximum demand and variations in lead time.

SALES MIX: the proportionate combination of the various products leading to a firm's total sales.

SALES MIX VARIANCE: a measure of the profit consequences of selling a combination of products in different proportions from the standard sales mix.

SALES QUANTITY VARIANCE: a measure of the amount of profit variance caused by selling more or fewer units than standard.

SEGMENTED REPORTS: reports that identify costs, revenues, profits, contribution margin, and other variables for segments of an organization.

SELLING PRICE: the dollar price that a customer must pay to purchase items.

SENSITIVITY ANALYSIS: a method of assessing the reasonableness of a decision that was based on estimates, testing the impact of differences from an estimate.

SERVICE DEPARTMENT: an organizational unit not directly producing goods but serving other departments.

SPECIAL ORDER: an order priced differently from the normal price in order to utilize excess capacity, thereby contributing to company profits.

SPENDING VARIANCE: the difference between actual manufacturing overhead costs and a flexible budget allowance.

SPLIT-OFF POINT: see Joint Production Costs.

STANDARD COSTS: an estimate of what costs would be under projected operating conditions.

STATEMENT OF CHANGES IN FINANCIAL POSITION: one of the basic financial statements in an annual report describing the financing and investing activities of an enterprise.

STOCK-OUT: something that occurs when all inventory has been used or sold.

SUNK COST: a cost already incurred that is now irrelevant to the decision-making process.

TARGET NET INCOME: a desired profit level predetermined by management.

TARGET PRICING: a means of setting prices to reach a profit objective.

TRANSFER PRICE: the price charged by one part of an organization for a product or service supplied to another part of the same firm.

UIC: Unemployment Insurance Commission (Canada).

UNDER-APPLIED OVERHEAD: the excess of factory overhead costs incurred over factory overhead costs applied.

UNFAVOURABLE VARIANCE: the amount by which actual dollar costs exceed standard costs allowed.

UNIT COST: the cost of producing and distributing one unit of a processed or manufactured item.

VARIABLE COST: a cost, uniform per unit, that changes in total in direct proportion to changes in total activity or volume.

VOLUME VARIANCE: the dollar amount of overhead variance caused by operating at an activity level different from the budget.

WORK-IN-PROCESS INVENTORY: the cost of all accumulated products that have entered the manufacturing process but have not been completed.

YIELD VARIANCE: the difference between the standard and actual output available from a given amount of inputs.